DIVINE *Thoughts*

Seeking Peace and a Sound Mind in a Chaotic World

DR. YOLLE-GUIDA DERVIL

Foreword by Marckdaline Johnson, MSW

Printed in the United States of America

Divine Beliefs Publishing Company
Dervil, Yolle-Guida

Divine Thoughts: Seeking Peace and a Sound Mind in a Chaotic World /Yolle-Guida Dervil. −1st ed.

ISBN-13: 978-0692790885
ISBN-10: 0692790888

10 9 8 7 6 5 4 3 2 1

While the author is a Licensed Marriage and Family Therapist and have provided the reader with ways to manage life circumstances, the material contained in this book are not intended as a substitute for seeking face-to-face therapeutic services from a mental health professional and/ or any other relevant professional for your specific needs.

DEDICATION

I dedicate this book to every restless soul that is seeking peace of mind… Every soul that is open to encounter a heavenly experience even in the midst of the chaos on earth. I dedicate this book to my younger, anxious self, your younger self, and all the young, precious souls that are aiming to make sense of this chaotic world. I dedicate this book to YOU! Your soul deserves PEACE—the peace that surpasses all understanding as the divine hand of God touches all 100 billion of your neurons connected to the trillions of synapses to produce a beautiful and peaceful connection of divine thoughts.

"For God did not give us a spirit of timidity or cowardice or fear, but [He has given us a spirit] of power and of love and of sound judgment and personal discipline [abilities that result in a calm, well-balanced mind and self-control" (2 Timothy 1:7, AMP).

Agape,

Guida

CONTENTS

ACKNOWLEDGMENTS

THANK YOU! MERCI! MESI! GRACIAS!

GRAZIE! DANKE SEHR!

I would like to thank first and foremost, God. You sent your own begotten Son to reconcile me with you. Jesus Christ, you died for me, so I would not have to pay for my wages of sin—death. I am forever grateful to you for rescuing me from myself. I thank you, Lord, for not only renewing my mind from the enslaved thoughts that kept me bound, but also for reviving my soul each day. Thank you for peace, thank you for love, and thank you for a second chance at life.

It was my first year in college, and I was over 200 miles away from family, friends, and my familiar habitat. I felt as empty as a rotted seashell, alone and washed up on the shore. I wanted life to end, and if it would not, I wanted to get off the world as it was rotating. I did not know how I was going to do it, but my mind tricked me into believing that the world would be better without me. What exactly was I adding to the world? Stress? Negative emotions? Once in a while, I would make somebody laugh, but only for a little while. Like a crack of thunder, the lies roaming through my mind became louder and stronger—until I got connected to a church community that showed me love and made me believe that life was worth living in Christ. I acknowledge my Pastor and Co-Pastor from undergraduate, Jerry and Eunice Parries. They were God-sent. They started the church at the university I was attending, right when I was seeking and searching intensively, attempting to make sense of life. I thank them for teaching me God's unconditional love and grace. I thank them for helping me discover my significance.

I also acknowledge my parents, Elie-Franc and Berenice Dervil who made me believe in the impossible. When the doctors said I would not make it, my mom prayed without ceasing and believed that I would not only live, but become a difference-maker. When society discounted me as a productive citizen, my dad embedded hopes, dreams, and aspirations in me to become the best version of myself. When I had lost hope in succeeding, my parents' high standards and belief in me aided me to push through despite the challenges of life. Their unconditional love, patience, and confidence gave me strength to continue the race of life.

To my beautiful maternal grandmother, my best friend, thank you for creating a safe space for me to share my thoughts with you. No matter how unorthodox my thoughts were, you made me feel comfortable enough to express them without judgment. Because of your acceptance of me, I was able to learn to accept and love myself. Thank you for your wisdom, your uninterrupted listening ear, and your constant reminder of how much I am loved and deserve the best.

To my amazing siblings, Cherlie and Cedrick Dervil, and my wonderful nephews, Jeremiah Jaheem Dervil and Elijah Vladimir Herard, I love you all. You are my strength, my inspiration, and my breath of fresh air. You all are the fuel to my fire. Thank you for showing an interest in the work that I do and encouraging me through the journey.

To my awesome aunts and uncles, who are second parents to me: Aunt Gisele, Aunt Anise, Aunt Brunette, Aunt Cereste, Aunt Rosemarie, Aunt Rose, Aunt Emile, Aunt Almaide, Uncle Idales, Uncle Wenson, Uncle Alexandre, Uncle Monfort, Uncle Enock, Uncle Enos, Uncle Chericie, and Uncle Ronald, I adore you.

To my family and friends, who continue to support me and encourage me throughout my journey of life, I love you all. There are too many of you to list, but you have especially assisted me in this last season of my life: Frantz Boileau, Wadson Theresias, Clara Merone, Danise Eldira, Lynndrell Washington, Joycelyne A. Bataille, Verna Popo, Sheriffa Wilkins-Colquhoun, Marckdaline Johnson, Angelynn Lindor, Kanya Wright, Sinnedy Cius, Martine Eldine, Darline Bonhomme, Andre Morris, Flavel Paul, Mirlande Francois, Paula Pierre, Juliana Deans, Sophia Rose-Lyn, Cheryl Rowe, Ilrose Charles-Saint, Guerda Jackson, Feediouse Duprat, Marita Hyppolite, Gwenda Cherelus, Getlyne Cherelus, Wadbert Duprat, Idanot Duprat, Roslet Duprat, Johnny Charelus, C.J. Noel, Daphnee Jacques, Dudlene Belizaire, Yanique Silvera, Rose Cherie, Natacha Bastien, Eddie Hicks, Lydia Hicks, Juanita Hunter, Danielle Spradley, Dominick Stokes, Nicole Joseph, Evaniel Francois, Stephanie Baptiste, Tracey-Ann Spencer, JoAnn Nyambura, Ronecia Duprat, Gabrielle Duprat, Ronald Duprat, Jr, Edwin Plancher, Getchens Plancher, Cindy Gonzalez, Jonhas Charelus, Rachelle Charelus, Camille Helm, Angela Rice, Marcela Henry Guzman, Natashia Lawrence, Schinell Johnson, Naz Ozaki, and Noemi

Fine. My ministry sisters: Lysa McMillan, Allegra Joffe, Linda Lee Marie Barraco, Dona Cespedes, Cierra Robinson, Kahla Elliston, Faith Scott, and the Tuesday Night Bible Study Group, and Camille Daly and the AXIOS: Thursday Night Single Ladies Small Group, thank you for holding me accountable in my relationship with God and helping me to study, digest, and apply the Word of God.

To all of my wonderful clients, thank you for granting me the privilege to walk through the darkest, yet most beautiful journey of your life.

To my editors: P.K.K., Lisa Cerasoli, Nicole Blake Johnson, Robert Infantry, Tracey-Ann Spencer, and Juanita Hunter, it really did take a village to make my scattered thoughts clear, understandable, and divine. Thank you for challenging my thoughts and stretching me to expound on my ideas. You all made this possible.

To everyone else who played a role in the exterior and interior of *Divine Thoughts*: my graphic designer, Doran Francis, book formatter, Dina, photographer, Ntebo Archer, makeup artist, Nora Emmanuel, thank you for turning an unattractive topic, such as defeated thoughts, and turning it into an appealing one. Please, forgive me if you have made a difference in my life and do not see your name.

Guida

FOREWORD

Every moment we breathe catapults us into another moment of our lives. For many of us, these moments are void of a definite sense of direction, understanding, wisdom, love, peace, or purpose. As a clinical therapist working in the State of Georgia and a Marriage and Family Therapy doctoral student with a Master's degree in Social Work, I find myself bombarded with anxiety and negative thoughts on a daily basis—from my clients, and often from me, if I'm not mindful of my thoughts and actions.

In this book, Dr. Yolle-Guida Dervil provides her readers with a comprehensive backdrop into her lived experiences with anxiety and mind battles. She uses questions and biblical references to aid readers transform hopeless thoughts to purposeful and peaceful thoughts. Dr. Dervil broaches the subjects of doubt, fear, anxiety, anger, sadness, and deeply rooted issues with great sensitivity and intellectual integrity; understanding that these moments of unmanaged (or mismanaged) emotional and mental health can penetrate and consume the thought process, consciousness, heart, soul, mind, spirit, and will of individuals challenged by the chaos of this world. As you ingest the material contained within *Divine Thoughts*, you will find that Dr. Dervil prescribes complex, yet profoundly simple ideas steeped in the peace of God. Hence, rather than circumventing this chaotic world, this book will take you through a thought-provoking and self-reflective process leading to a divinely mindful place. We all have access to this place.

Dr. Dervil lives a life purposed with others in mind. She makes it clear that she is unable to be who she has become without the divine faithfulness, intervention, revelation, grace, and mercies of God. Dr. Dervil believes changing old thinking patterns requires willingness to change, self-awareness, moment-by-moment dependency on God, honesty, and accountability. Beyond Dr. Dervil's scholastic achievements, she believes in community, and this is evident through her many undertakings: her nonprofit organization; her work with anti-human trafficking ministry; volunteering for one year as a live-in resident assistant with teenage foster boys, and another year as a live-in resident advisor for young women who aged out of foster care; leading/organizing weekly Bible studies, and more.

I recall meeting Dr. Yolle-Guida Dervil in 2010, during an internal practicum. She had a way of tracking personal and clients' thoughts by utilizing a method referred to as mind-mapping. In doing so, Dr. Dervil began her process of organizing her thoughts and those of her clients. As the years progressed, our academic, personal, professional, and spiritual journeys together offered me an eyewitness account of Dr. Dervil's life from anxiety-driven to mindful and authentic. Dr. Dervil's confidence and self-worth continues to grow as she seeks to manage her anxiety through transparency and implementation of God's Word.

Be encouraged and inspired as you read.

Marckdaline Johnson, MSW

CLIENTS' TESTIMONIALS

The process of learning how to restructure my thoughts has transformed my life. When I first came to see Yolle, I was full of chronic anxiety, fear, and negativity. I was mostly unaware of this; it had been going on for so long it seemed normal to me. Yolle helped me move past these issues by fully accepting God's love for me and learning to accept who I am and how God made me. I am now living a more positive, optimistic, grace-filled life. My thoughts are more peaceful and ordered, rather than confused and anxious. Prior to working with Yolle, I wasted much of my time and energy ruminating. Now, rather than doubting and questioning the work that God is doing in me, I am more fully trusting in God and moving in the direction of fulfilling His destiny for my life. Growing more and more into the image of Christ is a lifelong journey. I am thankful for the tools that Yolle has given me to help navigate it with gentleness, love, and grace. — ***J. S.***

I walked into Yolle's office, at D'Vin Therapeutic Services, skeptical. I had found her online, read about her a little, and even though I was apprehensive, I decided to reach out to her. I was in a dark place in my life, and nothing seemed to make the darkness go away. I had been to therapy before, several times, and often looked for a therapist that took a faith-based, Christian approach. This is part of why I walked into this particular session with doubt. The therapists I had seen before simply called themselves Christians. I initiated prayer time before our meetings. I initiated any mention about God. These sessions never seemed right, especially when I was asked or told things that seemed very contrary to my beliefs.

My first session with Yolle went as most sessions do. They ask about your life and why you are there. What made leaving this session different was that there was hope in my heart. Since that first meeting, I never wanted to stop going—until of course, it was time for me to move on from therapy. What I love about Yolle in particular is that she is *so* in tune with the Holy Spirit. She allows herself to be used by Him so beautifully. I am not a fan of beating around the bush or sugarcoating, and Yolle is so great at listening, but also knowing when to interrupt to make sure I was thinking and processing what I was saying. I never once felt like Yolle was trying to make me feel better by simply using words. Yolle made me feel comfortable. She made me feel like she really cared. It is so common for a Christian to tell someone that "God loves them." I had heard this several times before, and internally always thought, "Oh. Okay. That's cute." But when Yolle would consistently remind me, I actually believed her.

It has been over a year since I stopped seeing Yolle. I am not where I was when I first went to her, but I am also not entirely free from my thoughts, doubts, or fears. I am a huge believer that Yolle's goal, or a therapist's for that matter, is not to "free" you of whatever it is that is holding you back, but more so to be a guide to help you understand where certain issues come from, process them, and teach you how to navigate through them. If there is one thing that Yolle helped me understand, it was that this is a journey. Things don't just happen overnight, but if I allow the Lord to take a hold of my life, the journey is far more doable and satisfying. Today, my days are filled with fewer fears, doubts, and thoughts that attempt to drown me at all hours of the day. I don't know how differently my life would have played out if I had allowed my apprehension to keep me from reaching out to Yolle, but one thing I do know for sure is that part of who I am today, I owe to the Lord leading me to her. — ***G. L.***

We were truly blessed by our premarital counseling sessions with Dr. Yolle. One of our biggest obstacles was communication. One of the approaches we were taught was to listen to one another with the intent to understand, rather than looking to attack each other, by recognizing that we should learn to attack the problem and the enemy.

We learned to replace thoughts of trying to win an argument with thoughts of trying to come to some common ground. We were also taught on the importance of finances, and how handling money correctly is just one way for us to serve God. Dr. Yolle recommended some books for us to read to help this area of our life, as well. Since completing our sessions, our communication and financial planning has gotten a lot better. — ***Mr. & Mrs. A. W.***

PRAISE FOR DIVINE THOUGHTS

First, I would like to thank our Lord and Savior, Jesus Christ, for giving Dr. Yolle-Guida Dervil such boldness to share this book with us. During the years that I have known Dr. Dervil, I have found her to be a woman who wants to see everyone succeed. She has been faithful to the tasks that God has orchestrated her to accomplish.

Dr. Dervil has put into light, the truth, so that those who are captive can be set free. This is Dr. Dervil's first book, and I believe that many will be delivered through this book. *Divine Thoughts* is amazing and powerful. It is guaranteed to help you in every area of your life. This book reveals step-by-step revelation of the Word of God that breaks every restraint that you are dealing with in your life.

Divine Thoughts is a must-have if you plan on being successful, and if you desire to have an intimate relationship with God. Even if you are not a believer, this book is able to bless you and those connected to you.

– DR. CLARA MERONE
Advocate and Philanthropist

I believe it is by God's divine appointment that you are reading this inspirational book. It is undeniable that the core of human beings lies in their thoughts, for we are what we think. The goal of *Divine Thoughts* is to encourage the child of God to maintain divine thoughts according to the Word of God. The Word of God exhorts us: 'Finally, brethren, whatsoever things are true, whatsoever things are honest, whatsoever things are just, whatsoever things are pure, whatsoever things are lovely, whatsoever things are of good report; if there be any virtue, and if there be any praise, think on these things" (Philippians 4:8, KJV).

This is the only way to overcome the flesh, since our words and deeds are influenced by our thoughts. You will also experience peace and a sound mind when your thoughts are directed by the Holy Spirit. This divinely focused book will make an indelible mark on the way you think, and consequently impact your lifestyle as a minister of the Lord Jesus Christ shining your light in this dark world.

– DR. TRACEY-ANN SPENCER

Thought-altering, mind-altering, and life-altering, this book will help you recognize, acknowledge, and defeat those thoughts that are sent to rob you of your peace. Dr. Dervil's thought-provoking questions and exercises will force you to dig to the core of your mind. They will motivate you to uncover and uproot those distracting thoughts. They will set you free to focus on those things that are pure, noble, and true."

– VERNA POPO, ESQ.

Divine Thoughts is quite relevant, because so many individuals struggle with negative thoughts. I appreciate the truths that Dr. Dervil explored in her book as she guides us using many practical and biblical truths on how to have control over our thought life. 'As a man thinks, so is he,' Proverbs 23:7, has been a guiding principle for me for many years, since all we do and feel start in the mind. The 'Mind' is a 'Battlefield' for so many individuals, and as a Counseling Psychologist, I have worked with many individuals who struggle with negative and self-defeating thoughts which produce many mental and emotional disturbances. *Divine Thoughts* can be a great resource to help these individuals overcome and find peace of sound mind.

In addition, I appreciate Dr. Dervil's openness and transparency about her struggles with negative thoughts and how she victoriously overcame them. You, too, can overcome! Who would be better than Dr. Dervil to learn from about finding freedom from toxic thoughts and having peace of mind? I encourage you to read *Divine Thoughts: Seeking Peace and a Sound Mind in a Chaotic World.*

– DR. SHERIFFA WILKINS-COLQUHOUN
Author of *Secrets of Relationships*

Divine Thoughts is more than a book, but a guide on how to think about what is pure and what is true (Philippians 4:8-9). This book provides not only a practical method on how to meditate on scriptures, but also how to allow the Word of God to strengthen and breathe life into us. This book is a blessing and is needed for a time such as this. I thank you, Dr. Dervil, for allowing God to use you.

– ANGELYNN LINDOR
M.Ed. in Counseling Psychology

This book is a tremendous resource for those who want to walk victoriously and have divine thoughts. Dr. Dervil is thought provoking, honest, true, challenging, probing, and encouraging throughout her writings to help you gain peace in a chaotic world.

– ALLEGRA JOFFE
Licensed Residential Foster Parent

As the world progresses, people will experience more chaos, stress, and frustrations. And that is why *Divine Thoughts* will be essential to help people navigate through those obstacles. As a reviewer for this book, I learned to change my thought life because I applied the very steps that Dr. Dervil recommended. And they *work*!

– P.K.K
Editor

Divine Thoughts was so good for my soul. It is exactly what I needed to read, and I know that there are a lot of people out there right now that need to read this, too. It is for the fearful, the shamed, the despairing, the disturbed, the outcast, the worried, and the dry and thirsty souls who really need divine thoughts—which is all of us.

– STEPHANIE BAPTISTE
Founder and Owner of Inspired by Love Event Planning

INTRODUCTION

THE SIGNIFICANCE OF DIVINE THOUGHTS: SEEKING PEACE AND A SOUND MIND IN A CHAOTIC WORLD

In today's world, we are constantly inundated with different messages—good messages, bad messages, and even confusing messages—which influence our thought life, the way we process information. But the time has come to be more cognizant of the various messages that enter our minds. Although it is nearly impossible to filter every message, we can manage those that we entertain. Consider the barrage of internet pop-up ads that bombard us when we are online. Although we cannot always control what appears on our screens, we can control what we choose to click, connect to, and allow into our thought life. Similarly, as we go through our day-to-day activities, we must pay attention to what grabs us, and focus on how we choose to manage our thoughts on these activities. People average about 50,000 to 70,000 thoughts each day. With that many thoughts, it's easy to see why choosing to focus on victorious thoughts is best.

The Word of God instructs us to "Set your minds on things above, not on earthly things" (Colossians 3:2, NIV). This means that we should set our minds on things that are pleasing to God, rather than on thoughts that please ourselves and have no eternal impact. At times, we face challenges receiving and accepting the Word of God, due to the functioning of our brains.

Divine Thoughts will teach you how to restructure the way you receive and accept information, how to streamline your thoughts based on God's Word. Similar to how synapses bridge the gap between the axon terminals of two neurons to activate communication, God's Word bridges the gap between the truth of your existence and the dysfunction of your thought life. In order to exhibit good mental, emotional, and spiritual health, you will need to restructure your thought life. Reading and meditating on the Word of God daily will cultivate divine thoughts as you make it a habit. Below are biblical messages that will help to establish pathways in your life.

You are a child of God (John 1:12); you are a friend of Jesus (John 15:15); you are not your past (Romans 6:6); you are redeemed (Romans 3:24); you are a new creation in Christ (2 Corinthians 5:17); you have been set free (Galatians 5:1); you are blessed (Ephesians 1:3); you are forgiven (Ephesians 1:7); you have peace (Philippians 4:7); you are complete in Christ (Colossians 2:10)

Stream of Consciousness

I am certain that an authentic person is not exempt from mental health struggles; rather, they make a conscious effort to disengage from errors and inaccuracies of the past, become undaunted by the future, and live in the here and now. The peace and tranquility of life is found in the present moment. To stream our thoughts is to pay attention to what enters our minds and to be aware of how we respond to it. To stream our thoughts is to neither ruminate on the past nor be alarmed about the future, but to be present in the moment and to cherish every opportunity with peace and tranquility. It is in the here and now that we find peace of mind.

Our thoughts are the pathways through which we formulate ideas, opinions, and views of the world. Our thoughts determine the life we live every moment of the day. We can either choose to have divine, heavenly thoughts, or choose to have defeated, dreadful thoughts. Defeated thoughts block access to our spiritual and emotional pathways, causing disturbance in our lives. Consider the condition of your spiritual and emotional pathways and ask yourself: *How aware am I of my conscious experience moment to moment? How tranquil are the flow of my thoughts, even in the midst of chaos?* Analogous to streams of water that run smoothly around rocks in a calm river, God desires our thoughts to flow smoothly around the rocks of life. We do this by learning to exchange our own defeated thoughts with His thoughts, no matter the circumstances. This can occur by streaming your thoughts.

How do I gain this divine realization? Consciousness, or awareness of your thought life, will emerge as you adopt God's thoughts. The first step is to relinquish control of areas of your life that are unmanageable, and decide to allow God to govern your thoughts, your decisions, your communication, and your actions. If you are anything like me, initially you may find it difficult to surrender your thought life and adopt God’s thoughts. Although it is important to have your own thoughts, having divine, sacred thoughts is more important and beneficial to holistic wellbeing.

The benefits of having sacred thoughts are endless. Imagine hearing, receiving, and witnessing the most disturbing news but being able to flow past—like water around the rocks in a river—the detrimental thoughts and choose only beneficial ones to reflect on. Either you will believe that this newly discovered information will destroy you, or you will choose to believe that "rejoicing comes in the morning" (Psalm 30:5, NIV). This book has been designed as a guide to teach your mind to have divine, sacred thoughts from this moment forward. Just as a tenacious athlete trains to build and maintain strong, healthy muscles, we too must exercise our minds to develop divine thoughts.

Uncovered Veil

"He made known to us the mystery of his will according to his good pleasure, which he purposed in Christ" (Ephesians 1:9, NIV).

As you train your mind to exercise divine thoughts, God will reveal promises to you. Would you like to discover God's will for your life and learn how to start living an abundant one? The answer is yes for the majority of us, as we would not choose to deliberately live a life of defeat. I would like to share how my journey started—how I went from having constant anxiety to a state of inner peace as I discovered my identity in Christ.

At the age of seven, my innocent, childlike mind was exposed to a world of fear, confusion, and uncertainty. I was conditioned to think defeated thoughts, as I heard stories of wicked voodoo priests having power over people, as I witnessed envious individuals harming people simply out of spite. Prior to that age, my innocence was still intact. I saw beauty in the world, despite my constant hospital visits and a near-death experience. No one seemed to be able to properly diagnose my illness, which had me in a constant state of heaving and incapacitation. Family members often speculated it was due to evil spirits attempting to harm me. Yet, I prevailed over this sickness and the agony, poverty, and tribulations that existed from living in a third-world country. Life in the provinces of Haiti was difficult. However, as children, innocence often protects us from our surroundings. That was true for me until I turned seven. Unfortunately, the stench of death permeated my environment—not even a child's innocence can be protected from the venom of death's sting.

I still remember the day my brother took his last breath, right in front of my perplexed eyes. At that moment, I was not aware it was his last breath, that he had died, but somehow I understood that a tragedy had occurred. The room became dark, cold, and constricting. It was as if the earth stopped rotating, and I was thrown off balance. I felt like I was being crushed by an outside force, too—there was an overwhelming pain in my chest. I heard my mom wailing with words of anguish and hopelessness. That day was my introduction to death, in both its physical and emotional aspects. Not only did death come and rob my brother of life, but it also took my mother's peace—for years. Through that trial, I was also introduced to death's cousins: anger, anxiety, depression, distrust, and defeat. I had so many questions that went unanswered for years. I lived with constant doubt, fear of death, and anxiety about my future.

I always questioned why death claimed my brother, always wondering what that would mean for me. How could my brother die when I was the one constantly in and out of the hospital? Why my brother? If anyone was to be a victim of death, it should definitely not be my brother; it should be me. I thought I was the better candidate for such outcome, since everyone expected me to die. I was the physically weak and sick child. How could my brother die when he was the well-behaved one, and I the one causing my mother grief? How could my brother die when he was my life, my breath of fresh air, the one who made me feel whole and made me believe that I would feel well after throwing up, being rushed to the hospital, and getting spankings for misbehaving?

Fast-forward to a decade later, when anxiety chose to make my mind her permanent address. I was in the suffocating grip of paranoia, suicidal thoughts, and feelings of worthlessness. But the worst of it was that I managed to convince myself and others that I was okay, hoping that fear and anxiety would eventually vacate the premises of my mind. It was not until the death of my younger cousin (E.P.) that I decided I was no longer going to allow fear and anxiety to reign over my life. At that time, I was twenty-two years old and in the Marriage and Family Therapy Master's program in a private school in Fort Lauderdale, Florida. Since I was in a program that taught healing though psychotherapy, I decided to put aside my pride and seek therapy myself to manage my pain and grief. I was no longer in a position to hide my emotions. I was completely unhinged by then; my negative emotions were my own doing, and my classes started to suffer. Therefore, reaching out to a therapist was essential.

The therapy sessions revitalized my life. I felt as if my head were completely submerged in murky water on a hot, humid day, and I would only surface for air by the support of others. If I had not allowed myself to resurface, I would have drowned in my own defeated thoughts. Instead of accepting defeat in the many unresolved issues of my life, with the therapist's help, I cleared the debris—my fear and anxiety, unresolved problems, and defeated thoughts. This released some of the pressure from my mind and allowed me to breathe the fresh, calming air of hope. That experience was the beginning of my healing journey. That was my story. What about yours?

Take some time to reflect on what your unresolved issues are that continue to keep you bound and prevent you from completely trusting God at His Word. Many times, there is a stigma associated with a Christian seeing a psychotherapist. I am here to tell you, as a licensed Marriage and Family Therapist who has been seeing Christian clients for over seven years, that is a lie from the enemy. I beseech you, my brothers and sisters, take God at His Word, for His Word encourages us to seek godly counsel when it is needed (Proverbs 11:14, Proverbs 12:15, Proverbs 13:10, Proverbs 19:20, Proverbs 24:6).

My Personal Mission

Although I always knew my calling was to help others, going through my own therapeutic experience corroborated my role as a therapist. As a result, my aspiration is to share this great freedom and peace with others through my work and ministry. I feel like a person who has discovered a treasure of cool, rejuvenating spring water in a deserted land. Just as it would be a depravity to keep this clean, refreshing oasis a secret, it would be dissolute to not share these thoughts with you on how to obtain peace and a sound mind in a world filled with chaos.

"Do not withhold good from those to whom it is due, when it is in your power to act" (Proverbs 3:27, NIV).

I myself have implemented the concepts I write about in this book, and plan on continuing to practice divine thoughts daily. I also exercise the concepts with my clients, who have found it to be very valuable. I aspire to offer people practical ways to manage defeated thoughts as I challenge myself to help them uproot the core of their issues and avoid offering the simplicity of interventions. My personal mission is to "bind up the brokenhearted," proclaim freedom to those whose minds are in captivity, comfort all who mourn, and provide practical ways for people to find joy and peace as they walk through their journey or life (Isaiah 61:1-3, NIV).

So why is it important for us to have divine thoughts? Having divine thoughts will be a great return on investment in yourself. As a result, you can obtain a healthy mental life and gain peace of mind by restructuring your thought life. An added bonus is that you will save thousands of dollars from therapy sessions.

For the many years I have been seeing clients, I have worked with hundreds of people who lost control of their minds, or come close to it. My hope for you is that you understand and learn how to release some, if not all, of the pressures that life can bring. Intentionally train your mind to think about "Whatever is true, whatever is noble, whatever is right, whatever is pure, whatever is lovely, whatever is admirable—if anything is excellent or praiseworthy—think about such things. Whatever you have learned or received or heard from me, or seen in me—put it into practice [for your life]. And the God of peace will be with you" (Philippians 4:8-9, NIV).

In the pages to come, you will review various components of your thought life, and you will be challenged to explore ways you can realign any ineffective thought processes with God's. You will have time to pause, reflect, check your minds (mind checks), and have thoughts to consider. These are rest areas, opportunities to digest the information, rather than rush through it. If you suffer from anxiety, depression, mood disorders, or any other mental health condition, this book will help you a great deal. Nonetheless, I strongly suggest that you seek a licensed psychotherapist to help you through your condition(s). This book should by no means be a substitute for therapeutic services.

Pause:

Take three deep breaths. Allow your entire ribcage and abdominal muscles to feel each breath as you inhale through your nose and exhale through your mouth. Physically, these three deep breaths will trigger your parasympathetic nervous system to diffuse stress and elicit calmness. Spiritually, these three deep breaths have the power to allow the Holy Spirit to guide you through this journey of divine thoughts as you decide to allow each exhale to represent a release of defeated thoughts out of your body, and each inhale to represent peace and tranquility inside.

Choosing Peace

We have heard it said before: "Hindsight is always 20/20." Many people have made detrimental or unhealthy life choices due to being oblivious to the consequences of their actions. This often results in painful lessons and regrets. Examples are the reckless driver that caused the fatal accident involving multiple deaths, or the unfaithful father that was finally exposed and lost his entire family. Decisions are made continuously every day. Some are made with complete awareness, while others are from automatic responses to internal or external stimuli. In order to manage this chaotic world and live the abundant life that God has promised us, we must learn to have healthier mental states. As we go through a range of mental states that affect our daily decisions, let us set our minds to have divine thoughts, today and in days to come. Divine thoughts will result in better decisions, the ability to manage unexpected circumstances of life, and overall peace of mind.

Pause:

Take a moment to envision a life with the inconceivable gift of having 20/20 knowledge and awareness, without the pain of wondering the "What if?" Without thinking "If only I knew then, what I know now." What are some regrets that continue to haunt you, robbing you of your peace and sound mind? Today, start forgiving yourself and avoid having regrets. Regret is a disgraceful thief that robs you of your serenity. Choose peace and be shameless. Remember that there is no condemnation in Christ Jesus.

"Therefore, there is now no condemnation for those who are in Christ Jesus, because through Christ Jesus the law of the Spirit who gives life has set you free from the law of sin and death." (Romans 8:1-2, NIV)

How do we reach this peace of mind in a world filled with chaos? Is it fair to say that only the weak and vulnerable minds are susceptible to disorder and confusion? Is it factual that people can simply "think positive" through their struggles, contour their way to increase self-worth and experience happiness, and become more self-confident? I have encountered many individuals who believed that simply meditating, applying makeup, and going to the gym on a daily basis would fill the void without an overhaul of their thought life. In my years of counseling individuals from various walks of life, with various struggles ranging from acute mental illness to common family issues, I have come to realize that many of these struggles are deeply seeded, and can only be conquered by the daily renewal of one's mind.

Implementing those activities listed above does alleviate some of the pressure that many experience. However, oftentimes the benefits are short-lived. Hence our recidivism rate in the legal system, perpetual relapses with those who suffer from substance abuse and alcoholism, and our own repeated, unwanted behaviors. It is my observation that people are more likely to revert to their old habits if only brief interventions are applied and their minds are not renewed. When people learn to restructure their thought life and learn to establish new, healthy habits, they are able to maintain success.

Go through this journey of renewing and restructuring your thought life without rushing through the process. Take the time to learn how to rebuild it by applying the steps of divine thinking. When we encounter chaos, often we are told to seek resources that teach us how to "cope" with our emotions—counting to ten, hitting a punching bag, repeating affirmations. These interventions mentioned are effective in their own right, and they help our moods temporarily. However, there is long-lasting results when we seek to understand deep-rooted issues, which evoke change from the inside out. Continue reading to learn how to properly manage the thousands of thoughts that you filter through your mind on a daily basis.

Inside and Out

There is a misconception that our moods are correlated to external circumstances, such as the car breaking down, becoming unemployed, or receiving unpleasant news. Although these circumstances can greatly impact our mood and attitude, many of our emotions and the way we handle ourselves have more to do with our internal world, also known as the brain.

It is our internal world that shapes our external. For instance, many people have difficulty managing their moods, which can be due to unbalanced chemicals and physical health conditions. The attempt to handle one's internal state by merely focusing on the external circumstances is insufficient. I invite you to take this journey with me through your mind's neuropathways, but from a spiritual perspective. As we understand the mental conditions in which thought processes take place, we can win this fight over our thought life that leaves us paralyzed with fear, entangled with anxiety, engulfed with self-sabotaging actions, and lacking overall self-control.

In the secret place of your internal world, there lies an unseen battle in your brain that will be manifested through the external world if it is not managed by the renewing of your mind.

Will your thoughts remain true, pure, and comparable to Christ in the midst of uncertainty? To be honest, if you were to ask me this question four years ago, my answer would have been no. When life was not going my way, and I felt that God had forgotten about me, my mind started to believe the lies of the enemy more than I believed the promises of God. The key word is "felt." You see, I still believed in God. Yet my "feelings" and emotions were getting in the way of me completely trusting God at His Word. In John 10:10, we learn that "The thief comes only to steal and kill and destroy; I have come that they may have life, and have it to the full" (NIV). The reiteration states that "The thief does not come except to steal, and to kill, and to destroy. I [Jesus] have come that they may have life, and that they may have it more abundantly" (NKJV). That is how the enemy operates—he makes you forget God's instructions, and makes you believe that an abundant life is out of your reach. Whose word will you trust? Whose promises will you hold on to?

Thoughts to Consider:

The enemy, in this case, can be Satan or your own defeated thoughts. At times, we are our own worst enemy, and we tend to blame outside forces for our choices and behaviors. It is time to acknowledge our role in the consequences of our actions and learn to make better decisions by exercising a better thought life.

Reflection:

When faced with a quandary, ask yourself, "What role do I play in this situation, and how can I come out victoriously?" Remember, you do not have to be a victim of your circumstances. You can truly be victorious with Christ's help.

Take God at His Word

Are you ready to start training your mind to submit to the authority of God's foundational truths? His Word?

❖ God tells us to renew our minds daily, yet we continue to occupy our minds with the same depraved thought patterns.

❖ God urges us not to worry and be anxious for nothing, but we do the opposite. We worry excessively, until we become emotionally and physically sick from our ineffective thought life (Philippians 4:6).

❖ God instructs us to rejoice always, and again He says to rejoice. Instead, we ruminate on our struggles and life's circumstances (Philippians 4:4; 1 Thessalonians 4:16).

Reflection:

What happens when you hear a song over and over again? Most of us begin to memorize the lyrics and unconsciously think about the song. The brain is powerful; our unconscious mind registers information and brings it to our awareness so effortlessly. If our brains are able to do that with a song, how many more benefits would we receive if we were to trust God at His Word when He instructs us to meditate on His Word day and night? (Joshua 1:8; Psalm 1:2).

The benefits of meditating are endless. Meditation is a great method of relaxation. Spiritually and emotionally, it allows us to quiet the noises of our minds and intentionally reflect and engage in thoughts that promote stillness, calm, tranquility, and peace. God has promised us that if we meditate on His Word, and not on our own thoughts and the world's way of meditation, we will not only follow His steps, but also be prosperous and successful.

"Keep this book of the Law always on your lips; meditate on it day and night, so that you may be careful to do everything written in it. Then you will be prosperous and successful" (Joshua 1:8, NIV).

Before we delve into the specifics on how to have thoughts that are divine, I would like to show you that this journey is one that God has been waiting for you to take. He desires for you to live an abundant life, and the path to that abundant life is in His Word. As Christians, we often desire to receive the blessings and promises of God, but we do not put in the effort that He requires to follow His instructions on how to obtain them. Please do not get me wrong; God is a gracious God, and He will bless His children regardless of our actions. However, he values obedience (1 Samuel 15:22).

The Word of God is filled with promises, and if you are like me, you get excited when you read about the promises of God. When you read verses such as Proverbs 10:22, "The blessing of the LORD brings wealth, without painful toil for it" (NIV), you are ready to jump up and down for joy. However, what happens when the blessings have not manifested in your life, yet you continue to observe people around you receive them in theirs? Will you rely on your emotions, or have thoughts that are pleasing unto Him? In order to succeed in managing our thought lives even through disappointment, we must practice divine thoughts. Just as it is impossible for an athlete to meet his full potential without the proper training, it is nearly impossible for a Christian to experience the Kingdom of God on earth as it is in heaven, or the abundant life, love, joy, peace, patience, kindness, goodness, faithfulness, gentleness, and self-control without following God's instructions for living a Christian life (Galatians 5:22-23).

How do I start this journey, you ask? Let us examine Ephesians 4, as it will help us understand this process, and how it requires us to put away our old ways of thinking. The passage makes reference to the lives of Gentiles; in this case, a Gentile is someone who is living a life contrary to Christ's Word.

*"So I tell you this, and insist on it in the Lord, that you must no longer live as the Gentiles do, **in the futility of their thinking**. They are darkened in their understanding and separated from the life of God because of the **ignorance** that is in them due to **the hardening of their hearts.** Having lost*

all sensitivity, they have given themselves over to sensuality so as to ***indulge in every kind of impurity****, and they are full of* ***greed****. That, however, is not the way of life you learned* [21] *when you heard about Christ and were taught in him in accordance with the truth that is in Jesus. You were taught, with regard to your former way of life,* ***to put off your old self****, which is being corrupted by its deceitful desires; to be* ***made new in the attitude of your minds****; and to* ***put on the new self****, created to be like God in true righteousness and holiness"* (Ephesians 4:17-24, NIV).

As we review this passage, there are several foundational truths to consider. The first point is that our old way of thinking has been ineffective; therefore, we must think differently. Take this time to consider your thought life and how it has not served you well. For instance, I used to be governed by anxious thoughts: *I'm going to fail. What will "they" think of me? I cannot do it.* These defeated thoughts kept me from pursuing many great things, and almost kept me from publishing this book. But I give glory to God for granting me the strength to press on through, allowing me to apply divine thoughts to accomplish my goals.

Secondly, our hearts have been hardened, and we must seek God to soften them and make us receptive to The Holy Spirit. A hardened heart does not make room for God's wisdom and knowledge. A hardened heart clogs your spiritual pathways, which keeps you from hearing from God. Therefore, as you draw near to God by studying His Word and praying to Him, you will gain new understanding that softens your heart to receive His Word and His will for your life. His Word will give you consciousness and thoughtfulness, and keep you from **indulging in impurity** and everything else that is displeasing to God.

Through this passage, we learn that there is a new way of life. We must be open to discovering it through seeking God, by reading and listening to His Word and asking Him for strength to apply it in our day-to-day lives. This new way of life is all about Christ and how He came to save us from our sins. For me, He saved me from my selfish motives and defeated thoughts.

Thirdly, as we accept this new way of life, we will learn **to put off your old self**, which is being corrupted by its deceitful desires.

Mind Check:

What are some corrupted thoughts or deceitful desires you are currently battling?

___

___

___

How can you replace them with desires that line up with the will of God?

___

___

___

Lastly, as we reflect on the old self and how it is useless, we will learn how to adopt a new attitude of our minds and put on a new self. What does this new self, look like? The Word says we are "created to be like God in true righteousness and holiness" (Ephesians 4:24, NIV).

Pause:

In everything that you do and think, ask yourself, "Would God be pleased with this action or this thought?" The great news is that He understands that we cannot succeed in our thought life without His strength, and He is more than willing to provide us with strength and guidance. "Last of all, I want to remind you that your strength must come from the Lord's mighty power within you" (Ephesians 6:10, NIV).

Putting Off Your Old Self That is Corrupted by Deceitful Desires

As you seek to put off your old self, which is corrupted by deceitful desires, remember your thoughts become your actions and your actions become your character. But it all starts in the heart. So ask yourself, what is the condition of your heart?

"For as he thinketh in his heart, so is he" (Proverbs 23:7, KJV).

<table>
<tr><td>Old Thoughts:

"I'm not worthy."</td><td>New, Divine Thoughts:

I'm worthy of love and God loves me unconditionally.

"For God so loved the world, that he gave his only begotten Son, that whosoever believeth in him should not perish, but have everlasting life" (John 3:16, NKJV).</td></tr>
<tr><td>Hardening Heart:

"They do not deserve my forgiveness."</td><td>A Heart like Christ:

I forgive you, because Christ has forgiven me.

"For if you forgive men when they sin against you, your heavenly Father will also forgive you. But if you do not forgive men their sins, your Father will not forgive your sins" (Matthew 6:14-15, NIV).

"Bear with each other and forgive one another if any of you has a grievance against someone. Forgive as the Lord forgave you" (Colossians 3:13, NIV).

"Get rid of all bitterness, rage and anger, brawling and slander, along with every form of malice. Be kind and compassionate to one another, forgiving each other, just as in Christ God forgave you" (Ephesians 4:31-32 NIV).

"Therefore, if you are offering your gift at the altar and there remember that your brother has something against you, leave your gift there in front of the altar. First go and be reconciled to your brother; then come and offer your gift" (Matthew 5:23-24, NIV).</td></tr>
<tr><td>Ineffective Thoughts:

"I cannot do this."</td><td>Productive/Triumphant Thoughts:

I can and I will accomplish the plans God has for my life.

"I can do all things through Christ who strengthens me" (Philippians 4:1, NKJV).

"Commit to the Lord whatever you do, and he will establish your plans" Proverbs 16:3, NIV).

"No, in all these things we are more than conquerors through him who loved us" (Romans 8:37, NIV).</td></tr>
<tr><td>Impure Thoughts:

"I deserve to be happy by satisfying</td><td>Pure Thoughts:

My body is a temple of God, so therefore I will make every effort to not engage in anything that would give grief to the Holy Spirit.

"Do you not know and understand that you [the church] are the temple of God, and that the Spirit of God dwells [permanently] in</td></tr>
</table>

myself."	you [collectively and individually]? If anyone destroys the temple of God [corrupting it with false doctrine], God will destroy the destroyer; for the temple of God is holy sacred, and that is what you are" (1 Corinthians 3:16-17, AMP).

Mind and Heart Check: Your turn. Examine your thought life and the condition of your heart. As you engage in this exercise, ask God to reveal any unacquainted thought or heart condition that is displeasing to Him.

"Create in me a pure heart, O God, and renew a steadfast spirit within me" (Psalm 51:10, NIV).

Old Thoughts:	**New, Divine Thoughts:**
What is some of your old thinking that distances you from God? ____________________ ____________________ ____________________ ____________________	How do you think God would like for you to start thinking? ____ ____ ____ ____
Hardening Heart: What do you believe God is urging you to let go of? ____________________ ____________________ ____________________ ____________________ Who does He want you to forgive? (Don't forget about yourself.) ____________________ ____________________ ____________________ ____________________	**A Heart like Christ:** I will let go of: ____ ____ ____ ____ I will forgive: ____ ____ ____ ____

Ineffective Thoughts:	**Productive/Triumphant Thoughts :**
What are some defeated thoughts you have been experiencing? ____________________ ____________________ ____________________ ____________________	What do you believe you need to tell yourself to combat those defeated thoughts? ____ ____ ____ ____ What verses can you meditate on to have triumphant thoughts? ____ ____ ____ ____
Impure Thoughts: Are there behaviors that God has been asking you to cease from engaging in? What are they? ____________________ ____________________ ____________________ ____________________	**Pure Thoughts:** What steps do you believe you need to take to start living a life with pure thoughts? ____ ____ ____ ____

This is not your typical "think-positive-and-you-will- find-happiness" process!

Many have sold us this idea that we can just think positive thoughts and the "universe" will reward us with positive things. If you are like me, this has not always worked in your favor. When you are dealing with deep-rooted issues, the more you attempt to simply think positive thoughts, the more frustrating it becomes. Yes, having a positive outlook on life is valuable.

However, if you have lived long enough, you will discover that trials and tribulations are inescapable no matter how positive, wealthy, successful, and beautiful you are. Yes, I bring up beauty— this culture is so fixated on contouring and highlighting the face. Think about it; if simply "thinking positive thoughts" were that simple, why do many intellectuals continue to struggle emotionally?

Sigmund Freud was the neurologist and founder of psychoanalysis who came up with many theories on human personalities and behaviors. Although he stirred up quite a bit of controversy amongst his colleagues and professionals in his field, his knowledge and contribution to the field of psychoanalysis is noteworthy. Nevertheless, toward the latter part of his life, his theories were unable to relieve him from the tragic death he faced. To alleviate the intense pain from mouth cancer, Freud asked his doctor to administer a fatal dose of morphine, and his life ended.

Many others who were thought to be intelligent also ended their lives tragically. So one must wonder, why does the beauty queen continue to doubt her self-worth while being showered with admiration and accolades? And why has the spiritual leader continued to face moral failures, with all their understanding of right and wrong? Where does that leave us? Can we ever obtain true peace and experience true joy by having a sound mind? Absolutely! And the steps await you in these pages to come.

The journey of obtaining peace and divine thoughts can only be fully achieved with the help of the Holy Spirit. I pose this question to you: "Would you prefer to be a slave to the law or a slave to God?" Similar to Paul in Romans 7:15-25, I hope for us to choose to become a slave to God's law, for it is then you will rely on *God's* ways, not *your* ways. As you read through this book, I encourage you to be gentle with yourself. You will be provided opportunities to continue to reflect on divine thoughts in relation to your life. At times during your reflection, unpleasant emotions may be triggered. If your emotions become unmanageable, I strongly recommend for you to seek a licensed mental health professional.

The divine thoughts exercises are meant to help you become the best version of yourself. Please note that I strongly discourage self-condemnation. We have all fallen short of the glory of God (Romans 3:23); therefore, you will have moments where the very things you try to avoid are the very things you continue to engage in. Again, this is a process, and only the Holy Spirit will help you to be victorious with your transformation. Paul experienced the same struggle, and he shared it from Romans:

"I do not understand what I do. For what I want to do I do not do, but what I hate I do. And if I do what I do not want to do, I agree that the law is good. As it is, it no longer I myself who does it, but it is sin living in me. For I know that good itself does not dwell in me, that is, in my sinful nature. I have the desire to do what is good, but I cannot carry it out. For I do not do the good I want to do, but the evil I do not want to do—this I keep on doing. Now if I do what I do not want to do, it is no longer I who do it, but it is sin living in me that does it. So I find this law at work: Although I want to do good, evil is right there with me. For in my inner being, I delight in God's law; but I see another law at work in me, waging war against the law of my mind and making me a prisoner of the law of sin at work within me. What a wretched man I am! Who will rescue me from this body that is subject to death? Thanks be to God, who delivers me through Jesus Christ our Lord! So then, I myself in my mind am a slave to God's law, but in my sinful nature-a slave to the law of sin" (Romans 7:15-25, NIV).

What is Your Story?

Have you ever wondered why you engage in the very things you know you should not, knowing they are unhealthy for you physically and spiritually? Have you ever wondered how an individual can be indoctrinated into a particular system, whether it is a social, political, and/or religious system? The indoctrination can come through force, persuasion, manipulation, or from a person being "love struck," which results in that person abandoning his or her own belief system and attitude to undertake a completely divergent worldview.

Consider how Adolf Hitler was able to convince thousands of soldiers to conform to his political ideology, which resulted in genocide. What about a perpetrator of domestic violence? Let us name him MC, who is able to dominate the life of a well-educated, highly-motivated individual and convince her that she is worthless. In turn, she begins to doubt her own morals, beliefs, and sanity. And there is also DW, a beautiful, tall, young model with smooth skin and long, alabaster hair. But she has been struggling for years with body image issues. In addition to her diagnoses of anxiety and depression, she was recently diagnosed with Body Dysmorphic

Disorder (BDD). This mental illness has critically impaired the social, spiritual, occupational, and other significant parts of her functioning. She finds herself preoccupied with nonexistent or minor defects of her physical appearance. And we get to JB, a mother of five children from four different men. She constantly finds herself in unhealthy, destructive relationships clothed in what she labels as love. You see, at first glance, Hitler was well-liked, and then became one of the most feared and hated men by nations not only in his time, but generations after his death.

At first glance, MC appeared to embody endearing qualities—handsomeness, wisdom, and protectiveness. But he constantly exalts himself, and he is full of insecurities encased in arrogance. He demands his lady treats him like a king, worships him and abandons all—including herself—for him.

By nature of DW's profession, she would be expected to be confident, driven, and a role model for other young women striving for the same level of success. Nevertheless, many are unaware of the scars she carries from the years of emotional, physical, and sexual abuse she suffered as a child.

JB is the life of the party; she's "Ms. Popular." Her perceived reputation is a veil that covers her insecurity from dropping out in the tenth grade. She uses her body to obtain power, and the only way she compensates for her lack of love and security is when she is in a relationship, even at the expense of the safety of herself and her children.

Like Hitler, MC, DW, and JB, many of us appear to have it all figured out, with our great careers, robust personalities, and attractive smiles. However, if our deeper layers were examined, the same scars of unresolved pain, unexplainable anxiety, and unwanted insecurities would be discovered. In order to begin experiencing authentic peace and acquiring a sound mind, we must stop the pretenses and begin to dig deep into those areas of our lives that cause us to steer from God's commandments and conform to this world.

There is no one answer or formula to how we can avoid experiencing the effect of life's inescapable troubles. Nonetheless, I do believe that in order for us to manage inevitable consequences and maintain a sound mind, we must understand our thought life and begin to discipline our brains to submit to God's authority. The scenarios mentioned above are a small sample size of the various issues I have had to walk my clients through in therapy. I have come to realize that these individuals' circumstances were a result of an incident, and they then became victims of a defeated thought life. Like a successful athlete, we must learn effective strategies.

"All athletes are disciplined in their training. They do it to win a prize that will fade away, but we do it for an eternal prize. So I run with purpose in every step. I am not just shadowboxing. I discipline my body like an athlete, training it to do what it should. Otherwise, I fear that after preaching to others I myself might be disqualified" (1 Corinthians 9:25-27, NLT).

Pause:

At first glance, what would others think of you? Share how their opinions of you are either accurate or inaccurate.

____

____

____

What scars have you been hiding from those who are closest to you?

____

____

____

Get ready to embark on a life- and thought-changing journey that will enable you to become a champion of your mind. We will explore over thirty verses to support the restructuring of your thought life through the five Ps of transformation: Preparation, Positivity, Pruning, Perseverance, and Patience. In order for the pages in this book to come to life, you must decide to go through this journey with earnest intent to learn and grow, and a willingness to change your thought life as you let go of your own thoughts and exchange them with God's. Through fasting and prayer, and by the power of the Holy Spirit, endless possibilities await you on the other side of a liberated mind.

Pause:

By the end of this journey, how would you like your thought life to change?

____

____

____

List at least five negative, defeated thoughts that you would like to replace and identify the replacement thoughts:

Defeated Thoughts:	**Replacement Thoughts:**

Additional Notes:

____

____

____

____

____

Ready, Set, Go: Chapter Descriptions

"Be alert and of sober mind. Your enemy the devil prowls around like a roaring lion looking for someone to devour" (1 Peter 5:8, NIV).

Congratulations, you have gotten through the most difficult part of this journey, which is the pre-contemplation stage of change. You have pushed through the denial of thinking you can continue life by your own right, and you have instead become conscious of the need for a change in your thought life. According to Carlo C. DiClemete and J.O. Prochaska, two well-known alcoholism researchers, there are six stages of change when it comes to understanding addicts' problems and their level of motivation to change: pre-contemplation, contemplation, determination, action, maintenance, and termination. When it comes to overcoming an addiction or breaking an unhealthy habit, long-lasting changes are challenging to obtain.

Although you may not have an addiction to overcome, having a negative or defeated thought life results in similar consequences. Therefore, it requires much *preparation, positivity, pruning, perseverance*, and *patience* to be successful through this journey. Ultimately, it takes the help of the Holy Spirit to truly sustain long-lasting results. Going through the five principles listed above can help you identify unhealthy thought patterns, and to restructure and maintain a healthier more resilient thought life.

As you read through the preparation chapter, you will learn ways to prepare yourself through the learning phase of restructuring your mind. You will recognize who or what is getting in the way of your quest for divine thoughts, and you will learn strategic ways to overcome this battle. You will also become aware of practical ways to shield yourself as you go through the journey.

The second phase will consist of your taking your first prescribed dosage of divine thoughts—a cheerful heart sixteen times a day, and as needed. "A cheerful heart is good medicine, but a broken spirit saps a person's strength" (Proverbs 17:22, NLT). Additionally, you will focus on training yourself to restructure your thoughts from negativity and self-defeat to more positive, God-centered thoughts. You will learn how to reframe your thinking and have thoughts that are pleasing to God. You do so well cheering other people on, but yet you fail to get your own advice. You will practice asking yourself specific questions that will help you to develop this new habit as you learn the benefits of having God-pleasing thoughts.

The third chapter is when the work starts to get a bit challenging. This part of the journey will require complete transparency and honesty with yourself and the willingness to "kill your flesh," meaning to cut down areas in your life that are not pleasing to God and allowing other parts to grow and flourish. This phase of your journey may not feel good, since it requires letting go of the things that feel good physically, but not necessarily beneficial to your mental or spiritual well-being. But do not forget the previous chapter—stay positive and trust the process.

Perseverance is when you have decided that God's way is better, and that you have gotten too far to go back to your old ways. You will identify and meditate on scriptures that show ways to keep going and not grow weary in your walk.

Lastly, you will also learn the importance of being patient with yourself. In this journey, patience is vital. You will learn that you are human, and failure is part of the process. Nevertheless, exercising patience through the process is necessary. Through these five principles, I invite you to be transformed as we become more disciplined in renewing our minds daily. Ultimately, our hope is to have our minds set on Christ as we seek to live out His will in peace. This can only be achieved through Christ. Outside of Christ's strength, we cannot obtain pure, divine thoughts.

"And be not conformed to this world: but be ye transformed by the renewing of your mind, that ye may prove what [is] that good, and acceptable, and perfect, will of God" (Romans 12:2, KJV).

PART I
PREPARATION

Chapter One

A SHIFT IN PERSPECTIVE

"By controlling the direction of your mind, you control the direction of your life."
— Dr. Caroline Leaf

For every task that you expect to complete, it is recommended you properly prepare. As you seek to have divine thoughts, it is important to ready your mind to be trained to handle any and all thoughts and circumstances that are encountered. A person who properly prepares is a wise person. Take the parable of the ten virgins, for instance:

"Then the kingdom of heaven will be like ten virgins who took their lamps and went to meet the bridegroom. Five of them were foolish, and five were wise. For when the foolish took their lamps, they took no oil with them, but the wise took flasks of oil with their lamps. As the bridegroom was delayed, they all became drowsy and slept" (Matthew 25:1-5, ESV).

The parable went on to say that the five foolish virgins did not properly prepare for their journey to meet with the groom; therefore, they missed the privilege of being a part of the wedding feast. They traveled with lamps, which indicates that they were traveling at night and needed the light to guide their pathways. Avoid being like the foolish virgins, and be intentional in learning effective ways to exercise divine thoughts.

As you begin this journey, consider how much oil you will need in your lamp as you travel. We often travel in dark places, and like the ten virgins, we need our lamps. In this case, our lamp is God's Word. "Thy word is a lamp unto my feet, and a light unto my path" (Psalm 119:105, KJV). How much oil will you have? Imagine oil as your anointing (Exodus 30:30-32) and your anointing as the Holy Spirit (Galatians 3:26). As mentioned previously, the Holy Spirit plays a vital role in our success in having divine thoughts.

Pause:

If you are currently facing a situation, how much oil are you working with?

____

____

____

____

____

Are you in need of more oil to get you through your current situation? Take the time to ask the Holy Spirit to replenish your lamp.

____

____

____

____

____

Now that you have chosen to learn how to properly prepare yourself to obtain a sound mind, let's discuss what it really means to have a sound mind. Having a sound mind requires a shift in perspective. This mind that we have exists autonomously, as it is a world of its own. Since the early periods of history, many have attempted to make sense of the brain—a three-pound, wrinkly, walnut-shaped mass that human beings carry in their heads. It is humbling to consider how we have been able to travel to space, clone animals, and determine the sex of an unborn child, but we cannot seem to completely figure out the very organic matter that allows us to function. Within our brains, we have minds that manifest our views and perception of the world and our thoughts, emotions, and overall experiences. To understand our brains is to understand our thought life. However, we take comfort in knowing that understanding God and trusting His perfect will is enough to follow His instructions on how we should think. Praise be to God, the author and finisher of our faith, the Creator of heaven and earth, Alpha and Omega, Lord of lords, and King of kings. He has instructed us to trust Him, that His ways are higher than our ways.

"'For my thoughts are not your thoughts, neither are your ways my ways,' declares the LORD. 'The heavens are higher than the earth, so are my ways higher than your ways and my thoughts than your thoughts" (Isaiah 55:8-9, NIV).

Although we cannot fully comprehend God's ways, and we are left with more questions than answers, I encourage you to trust that everything God has created is beautiful, including your thought life. We must not fear our minds, for a liberated mind with thoughts like Christ is a beautiful mind. Scriptures have reminded us that "He has made everything beautiful in its time. He has also set eternity in the human heart; yet no one can fathom what God has done from beginning to end" (Ecclesiastes 3:11, NIV).

Pause:

List any questions you have that affect your thought life. Once listed, ask God to reveal the answer to you. Trust that His ways are higher than our ways.

____

____

____

____

____

For countless years, human beings have attempted to make sense of this complex world. If we want to win this battle over our thought life, we must understand who or what we are fighting. To properly prepare to have a sound mind is to understand our opponent.

"For our struggle is not against flesh and blood, but against the rulers, against the authorities, against the powers of this dark world and against the spiritual forces of evil in the heavenly realms" (Ephesians 6:12, NIV).

So then, how do we overcome these struggles? In this case, our struggles are our defeated thought lives. You may have believed that these negative, defeated thoughts had something to do with bad habits in the way we think. But according to the scriptures, there are forces operating against you and me in the spiritual realms that are influencing our thought life. Remember, "The thief comes only to steal and kill and destroy; I have come that they may have life, and have it to the full" (John 10:10, NIV).

These battles are inevitable and inescapable. I once heard a pastor describe our human experiences as such: "We are either going through a storm, coming out of a storm, or getting ready to enter a storm." Either way, you will be faced with a storm. It would be unwise for us to know that a natural disaster arising, but fail to properly prepare. Similarly, it would be unwise of us to know that in life there will be tribulations and that God has given us tools to overcome them, but not take full advantage of the preparation process. Satan's ultimate plan is to steal, kill, and destroy our thought life until we take our last breaths. Thus, in preparing our thought life, we must be reminded that the battle is spiritual. We must recognize and acknowledge the opponent whom we are fighting against. The great news is that Jesus has already defeated Satan. Satan is a thief of many things, and he comes to steal our joy and peace of mind, but we are protected when we prepare our minds and set them on Jesus.

In preparing to win over our thought life, we must understand the rest of the scripture.

"[13] Therefore put on the full armor of God, so that when the day of evil comes, you may be able to stand your ground, and after you have done everything, to stand. [14] Stand firm then, with the belt of truth buckled around your waist, with the breastplate of righteousness in place, [15] and with your feet fitted with the readiness that comes from the gospel of peace. [16] In addition to all this, take up the shield of faith, with which you can extinguish all the flaming arrows of the evil one. [17] Take the helmet of salvation and the sword of the Spirit, which is the word of God" (Ephesians 6:13-17, NIV).

Pause:

Before continuing, let us take some time to digest this passage. For some, reading this passage can be a bit abstract. It can be difficult to understand exactly what the Holy Spirit is asking you to do. I am inviting you to pray and ask God to reveal what He would like you to take from these verses.

Prayer: Father Lord, please help us to make sense of this passage. Help us to understand how this can apply to our own lives. In Jesus's name.

Go back and read the passage again. Ask yourself, "What does this all mean—putting on armor, belt of truth, breastplate of righteousness, Gospel of peace, shield of faith, helmet of salvation, sword of the Spirit?" You may start realizing that this is war. Yes! You are correct—you are in a spiritual war, and you will come out victoriously when you approach it from a spiritual perspective.

The *Full* Armor of God

When a soldier prepares for a battle, he does not wait for the enemies to get close for him to put on his uniform. He has his full battle gear on, ready to fight. Likewise, we must put on our full armor: the belt of Truth (Ephesians 6:14); the breastplate of Righteousness (Ephesians 6:14); the Gospel of Peace (Ephesians 6:15); the shield of Faith (Ephesians 6:16); the helmet of Salvation (Ephesians 6:17); the sword of the Spirit (Ephesians 6:17).

Truth:

The Word of God is truth. How much of the Word of God do you have inside you? The world has a postmodern way of thinking that tells us that there is no truth and that everyone's perception is their reality.

Challenge yourself to read the Word of God daily. Study to show yourself approved (2 Timothy 2:15).

Righteousness:

As you read God's truth/His Word, you will discover what He is pleased with.

Mind Check:

Identify three thoughts you are entertaining that are displeasing to God.

1. ____

2. ____

3. ____

What steps can you take to replace those displeasing thoughts with more righteous ones?

____

____

____

____

Steps to Prepare for a Sound Mind

1. **Know Whom You Are Fighting:** Recognize that you are not fighting yourself or those around you; you are fighting Satan, who comes to kill, steal, and destroy your thought life. Next time you have one of those negative, defeated thoughts, be reminded that Satan is roaming in the atmosphere near you. Tell yourself, "No, I will not fall prey to Satan's schemes." Pray for God to help you to change the thoughts.

2. **Kill Your Flesh Daily:** What is our flesh, and what does it mean to kill it? Our flesh is the desires of the world, and anything that goes against God's desire for you, such as lying, jealousy, and sexual immoralities. To kill our flesh is to deny our desires that are contrary to God's Word, and instead accept His desires. Whenever you have a desire or craving to curse a driver who just cut you off, lie to your boss about being tardy, or cheat on your spouse to fill a void in your life, pause and reflect on how this would only be a temporary pleasure with lasting negative consequences. This will be reviewed further in chapter three.

3. **Take Up the Whole Armor of God**: This simply means that you have to pick up your Bible daily and read it. In order to be prepared for the inescapable battles you will face in life, take a further step—don't just read your Bible, but apply it.

4. **Stand Firm**: Trust and believe that God has already won your battles for you. You are already victorious with your thought life; you just have to stand firm and believe it. Do you believe that? If not, take some time to confess to God that you are not taking Him at His Word. Although you may believe Him in some areas of your life, pause and reflect on how you can trust Him in all areas of your life. Like the boy's father in Mark 9:24 (NLT),

pray this simple, yet powerful prayer: Lord, "I do believe, but help me overcome my unbelief!"

Pause:

Based on what you have read, how will you prepare yourself for a sound mind?

____

____

____

____

What steps will you take to put on the *full* armor of God?

____

____

____

____

Now that you have a better understanding of what you are faced with—fighting against rulers, authorities, the powers of this dark world and the spiritual forces of evil in the heavenly realms—let's review how that understanding can help you to avoid the enemy's schemes in tempting you to conform to this world.

"Do not conform to the pattern of this world, but be transformed by the renewing of your mind. Then you will be able to test and approve what God's will is—his good, pleasing and perfect will" (Romans 12:2, NIV).

You have probably heard or read this verse countless times, but ask yourself, "Have I listened to God and accepted His instructions from this verse?" He has giving us clear commands on how to renew our minds. The first instruction is for us not to conform to this world. What exactly does this mean? To conform to a particular system is to comply with their practices and way of life. The world's standards differ from God's standards. Therefore, when you are examining whether or not you are conforming to the world, ask yourself, "Is my behavior in accordance with the Word of God, or with the world's standards?"

Once you have chosen to avoid conforming to the world, the next step is to renew your mind. In order for something to be renewed, there must have been damage, impairment, or discontinuation of an activity. For instance, if a person's membership at a gym has expired, he or she will have to **renew** it in order to continue services at that gym. A doctor may have to **revive** a patient after he or she loses consciousness. A couple may have to **restore** their relationship after losing trust due to unfaithfulness. An athlete may have to **recover** strength to compete, after coming out of leg surgery. An individual who has conformed to this world now has to take time to readjust his mind to a new system, which is God's system. For people to renew their minds, they must first recognize that their way of thinking is damaging to their spirit. They must introduce their minds to new thoughts that are in line with God's principle of living (Ephesians 4:1-32).

Our minds have been damaged by the world's methods, and God is calling us to renew, revive, restore, and recover our minds—daily. Here are a few examples of how you can renew your mind daily: Read His Word, meditate on it, and write journal entries and reflect on the positive things that are happening in your life.

Pause:

It is your turn to come up with examples of how you will renew your mind daily. From this day forward, what daily steps will you take to renew your mind?

____

____

____

____

We have learned that to properly prepare ourselves to have a sound mind, we must first renew our minds. Once you have renewed your mind, you must then protect your mind. Pay attention to what you are allowing to enter into your system.

Mind Check:

Ask yourself, “What am I allowing my mind to be exposed to?” (TV shows, music, negative thoughts, and unhealthy relationships). List your distractions below and identify how they are impacting your thought life.

____

____

____

____

Reflection:

“Faith comes from hearing the message, and the message is heard through the Word about Christ” (Romans 10:17, NIV). Are you hearing enough of the Word of God, or are you hearing more from the world? Prepare yourself to receive God by exposing yourself to His Word. Will you hear God when He instructs you which way to go, or will you be too preoccupied from the world?

Guided by The Holy Spirit:

In order to successfully handle life’s unforeseen circumstances, you must listen closely to the Holy Spirit. Are you ready to listen and allow God to guide you? "But keep on the alert at all times, praying that you may have strength to escape all these things that are about to take place, and to stand before the Son of Man" (Luke 21:36, NASB).

Mental Exercise:

Just as some people spend hours at the gym to build muscles, this journey will offer us an opportunity to strengthen our brain muscles. For the next seven days, document what you feed your mind and how. Are you feeding your flesh or your spirit?

Chapter Review: To prepare ourselves for a renewed mind, we must do the following things:

A. Shift our perspectives by deciding to think thoughts that are in agreement with God’s principles.
B. Pay attention to what we are feeding our minds.
C. Wisely choose what we allow to enter our minds.

PART II
POSITIVITY

Chapter Two

THE PURSUIT OF ~~HAPPINESS~~ JOY

"A joyful heart is good medicine, but a crushed spirit dries up the bones."
Proverbs 17:22, NASB

Now that we have prepared our minds and spirits to obtain a peaceful and sound mind, we must remember that a positive mindset is as crucial in maintaining that paradigm shift to adopting God's thoughts over our own. Having a positive state of mind does not mean you are oblivious to the world around you, nor does it mean you overlook unpleasant experiences. Having a positive worldview simply means that you decided to reframe the way in which you see, feel, and deal with unpleasant or painful events that you encounter throughout life. Thus, you have chosen to exist in peace and joy. When peace and joy are present, they welcome positive thoughts, and you are able to maintain your thought life.

At this point of your divine thoughts journey, we will expose and explore old habits of defeated thoughts that are robbing you of your peace and leaving your spirit bruised. As you excavate the times when your thoughts were less than positive, you will be able to understand how to bring positive thoughts to the forefront of your mind. I will share practical ways to mold your brain to go to thoughts that are more cheerful and victorious in nature. This reframing process will take place by consciously choosing thoughts that are pleasing to God, which builds and strengthens your spiritual neuropathways. In turn, it will reinforce your psychological neuropathway. Ultimately, the purpose of restructuring your thought life is to live and experience the abundant life that Jesus Christ came to the earth to offer us (John 10:10).

Examination of Old Habits

Through countless therapy sessions I conducted, I discovered a common thread with my clients working through anxiety: they too often ruminate on a thought, situation, or belief for much longer than necessary. When I ask them how ruminating brings them peace and joy into their life, they admit that it brings no positivity and only increases their level of anxiety, causes pain and frustration, and stifles their thought life. As we work through the anxiety, the client soon realizes they are hung up by a defeated thought life. The primary goal is to help them examine their old habits of thinking. I often ask them to create a detailed list of all of the defeated thoughts that filter through their minds on a daily basis (for some, by the minute).

The list usually overwhelms them by the time it is completed. I then ask them to write down the negative effects their defeated thoughts have in their lives. We spend some time examining and processing all the components of their list. Common defeated thoughts I have addressed with clients are struggles with accepting past failures, feeling remorse, inability to manage current responsibilities/expectations, and fear of the unknown.

One may wonder how it is that a person can continue to have these negative thought patterns, while also knowing the negative impact those thoughts have in their lives. Although such a choice may be absurd to some, it is a very justifiable option to others. The human brain responds to unpleasant experiences very differently than it does to pleasant ones. Hence, a person may not remember an exciting trip to Disney World when he was five, yet that same individual is able to recall a sexual abuse experience at the age of three and continues to have flashbacks of the experience into adulthood. Because our brains are hypersensitive to negative experiences, that should not be alarming. Fortunately, we can do something about the way we process information, and change defeated thoughts into victorious thoughts. We are all created with different levels of tolerance to unpleasant situations. Gracefully, we are not the sum total of our thought life; we are new creations, including our brains, our minds, and our thought life. "Therefore, if anyone *is* in Christ, *he is* a new creation; old things have passed away; behold, all things have become new" (2 Corinthians 5:17-21, NKJV). Let this foundational truth motivate you to continue this journey of restructuring your thought life from negative and defeated to more cheerful, joyful, and victorious.

Mind Check:

Defeated thoughts can suffocate us from breathing the fresh air of new forgiveness that God offers us daily. Today, choose to reject the lies that your mind often tricks you to believe. Be motivated to take actions and start embracing your desired thoughts and the positive effects they will have on your quality of life. Take some time to pause and reflect on old habits that rob you of peace and joy. Consider the desired thoughts that will help you start formulating new, healthy, and happy thoughts.

Spiritual Neuropathways — Divine Thoughts

Our thoughts are words we give meaning to, filtered from learned behaviors and personal experiences. These thoughts then shape our belief system, which then shapes behaviors. In order to build and strengthen our psychological and spiritual neuropathways, we must explore our thoughts and the meaning and experiences attached to them. Once identified, we must then replace any negative, defeated thoughts with divine ones.

Breaking Old Defeated Thoughts and Forming New Divine Thoughts

Defeated Thoughts	The Negative Effects of Those Thoughts	The Desired Thoughts	The Benefit of New Thoughts	Steps Required to Obtain New Thoughts
1. I'm not worthy of love. 2. I can't do it. 3. I'm to blame. **Now your turn:** 4. 5. 6.	1.You're robbing yourself from receiving love. 2.You're suffocating your mind with lies. 3.You're drowning yourself with guilt. 4. 5. 6.	1. I want to be loved and give love. 2. I can do it. 3. It was not your fault. 4. 5. 6.	1. You will allow your mind to accept love. 2. You will do it. 3. You will learn to forgive yourself. 4. 5. 6.	1.Create opportunities to be loved. 2.Take actions and just do it! 3.Learn to be gentle with yourself by letting go of past mistakes/failures & tragedy. 4. 5. 6.

"Folks are usually about as happy as they make up their minds to be."

—Abraham Lincoln

Joyful Choosing

It is fascinating how the above quote came from a man whose life was riddled with trials and unhappiness, but who refused to cave into the death grip of sadness. As I researched Abraham Lincoln's journey in life, I came to realize that he deliberately chose to be in a consistent state of positivity in the midst of adversity. I often wonder how many people would have chosen a positive attitude and mindset while going through difficult times. Could you choose positivity after losing your mother at the age of nine, experiencing financial instability and career rejections, losing three of your four children, and being married to a mentally unstable spouse, all while being responsible for the safety and well-being of your country during the most challenging time of your presidency? Then, he was assassinated at the ripe age of fifty-six. Was it worth it? I am confident that President Lincoln would have boldly responded, "Yes!"

Who is better to teach us the importance of choosing happiness over sadness than the sixteenth President of the United States? President Lincoln led the United States of America through its Civil War, abolished slavery, and strengthened the U.S. government; in the same way, we should strive to live a life that inspires and strengthens others by our positive outlook and choices in life. We should seek to eradicate hopelessness. Choosing positivity may seem an unattainable goal, but it is within reach. I am sure that none of the slaves saw the end of slavery, and yet it was abolished.

The Restructuring Process

Although our brain is a very complex and intricate machine to understand in its entirety, it is easily manipulated. For instance, we are able to visualize an opportunity and trick our bodies to believe our brain prior to succeeding in that activity. Take, for instance, a runner that is close to the finish line. Physically, this athlete may want to stop running. However, the secretion of endorphins fuels their stamina by simply envisioning the positive outlook of winning.

Positive thinking is very powerful, and the more we train our brain to focus on the positive outlook of life, the more positive outcomes we will have. Success in life hinges upon restructuring the brain to believe in success, even if it may seem impossible at times. Restructuring your brain from having defeated thoughts to positive and conquering will require persistent repetition. Constant application of a process brings about greater results. Therefore, it is vital for us to be aware of what we are ruminating on. Either you are meditating on thoughts that bring about positive feelings, or you are replaying the thoughts that create anxiety in your life. As mentioned previously, the more we hear a song, the more we will memorize and regurgitate the lyrics. Imagine if FEAR (False Evidence Appearing Real) were a song; all of the negative lyrics or messages from the song would permeate your thoughts. The more you play the song of fear, the more you will begin to think of those undesirable lyrics. A more specific example is when you are driving and get stuck in traffic. While in traffic, you are listening to songs with aggressive lyrics, and before you notice, you are upset and quick-tempered with others.

Pause:

You have the opportunity to saturate your mind with pure, lovely, and admirable thoughts. Challenge yourself today to replace defeated, fearful thoughts with ones that are more pleasing and uplifting to your spirit.

Changing the Lyrics: Creating a New Tune through Meditation

Now imagine if peace were a song. "Let go and let God," the lyrics say. "Tranquility is at your fingertips. It is possible to experience joy and a sound mind." The more you meditate on those words, the more your mind and heart will receive and believe them. God is calling us to meditate on His Word, not only when we are in time of need, but day and night. Call unto the Lord all of the time, not just most of the time.

Mind Check: Write a new tune that you will sing to invite positive, peaceful thoughts:

____

____

____

____

Reminder Verse:
"Keep this Book of the Law always on your lips; meditate on it day and night, so that you may be careful to do everything written in it. Then you will be prosperous and successful" (Joshua 1:8, NIV).

Caution: Fragile
Be Gentle with Yourself

I am in awe of the kind and nurturing we show towards others, especially children, but we struggle with showing the same kindness to ourselves. It is as if we close the door on our own lives. We would not dare say disparaging statements to children about their drawing or singing voice. How is it that we are so positive with other individuals, but so rough with ourselves? As you continue to restructure your thought life, it is important to remember to handle yourself with the same tenderness that you do others, similar to the way we would attend to the emotion of an innocent child.

Pause:

In order to be successful at restructuring our thoughts, it is important to meditate on harmonious thoughts to help us succeed in having a victorious thought life.

Mental Exercises:

Memorize the verses below, and when your thoughts are becoming negative, meditate on the verses. In addition to the verses below, identify your own verses that will aid in changing your thoughts from negative to positive.

"For though we walk in the flesh, we are not waging war according to the flesh. For the weapons of our warfare are not of the flesh but have divine power to destroy strongholds. We destroy arguments and every lofty opinion raised against the knowledge of God, and take every thought captive to obey Christ" (2 Corinthians 10:3-5, ESV).

"Rejoice in the Lord always; again I will say, rejoice. Let your reasonableness[a] be known to everyone. The Lord is at hand; do not be anxious about anything, but in everything by prayer and supplication with thanksgiving let your requests be made known to God. And the peace of God, which surpasses all understanding, will guard your hearts

and your minds in Christ Jesus" (Philippians 4:4-7, NIV).

"May these words of my mouth and this meditation of my heart be pleasing in your sight, Lord, my Rock and my Redeemer" (Psalm 19:14, NIV).

"May my meditation be pleasing to him, as I rejoice in the Lord" (Psalm 104:34, NIV).

Your Thoughts vs. God's Thoughts

Now that we have explored our defeated thoughts and learned how to restructure them through meditation, the focus remains on God's specific steps for us on how to succeed at having a positive thought life. There are eight key pillars we must focus on to win this battle to achieve a positive mindset: truth, honesty, justice, purity, humility, pleasant report, virtue, and praise. No matter what the obstacle we are presented with in life, the way in which we react will determine our outcome. The best way is to approach every circumstance with a positive, Godlike attitude.

Having suffered from anxiety since the age of seven, I have personally implemented the concepts mentioned above. As mentioned before, I have also walked through the steps with my clients, and they found them advantageous. As you read through the eight pillars, there will be reflective questions posed. I invite you to say these concepts out loud. They require active participation. I have learned that self-talk is beneficial in overcoming defeating thoughts. As you speak the truths out loud, your brain will be able to register your voice, which resonates to your heart to submit to them. When examining defeated thoughts, determine if the thoughts merit the energy you are giving to them. Also determine what you can do about it, or if it is a situation best relinquished to God. We can only manage the situations that we have immediate control over, and the situations we do not, we must give to God.

I challenge you to be honest with yourself as you answer the questions below and avoid rushing through them. This is also not a one-time process; it can be repeated as often as necessary. If you answer no to any of the questions, that issue needs to be buried at the feet of the cross—meaning that the situation needs to be left far from your thoughts, denied from being allowed to reenter your mind. It is to be buried once and for all—not for a couple minutes, not for a couple hours or a few days, but forever. You are prohibited from rehashing that experience.

Questions, based on Philippians 4: Consider a current situation, and let's practice how to have divine thoughts rather than defeated thoughts.

❖ Self, are my thoughts on this presented situation **true**? If the answer is no, bury it!

❖ Self, is the way that I perceive this presented situation and the potential outcome an **honest** way of going about it? If the answer is no, reconsider your perception and what is more authentic.

❖ Self, is my mindset on this presented situation **just**? Is it fair for me to continue to think of it the way that I currently am? If the answer is no, shift your focus and be more reasonable with yourself.

❖ Self, is the way that I am experiencing this presented situation **pure**? If the answer is no, seek God for cleanliness of thoughts.

❖ Self, is the way that I am viewing this situation **lovely** or pleasant? If the answer is no, ask God to help you see the beauty in every circumstance.

❖ Self, is the way that I am analyzing and explaining this situation to myself and others of **good report** (accurate and true)? If the answer is no, practice speaking life with every breath that you take. Consider the power that your tongue has, which is life and death (Proverbs 18:21).

❖ Self, is the way I relate to this presented situation **virtuous**? If the answer is no, shift your focus and consider the benefits of experiencing this situation in an honorable way.

❖ Self, does the way that I speak of this situation bring God **praise**? If the answer is no, ask God to help you learn how to praise Him in all your circumstances, good or bad.

Pause/Prayer:

LORD, since I have one or more answers that are no, please help me to think of my present situation with truth and honesty, and with a pure, lovely, and virtuous mind. When I speak of this situation, help me to share the good report so that it will be praiseworthy of sharing.

Mind Check/Prayer:

Mind, I refuse to allow you to be imprisoned by negativity. Today, I decree and declare that my thoughts will be thoughts that align with Philippians 4:8. Amen!

Philippians 4:8: "Finally, brethren, whatsoever things are **true**, whatsoever things [are] **honest**, whatsoever things [are] **just**, whatsoever things [are] **pure**, whatsoever things [are] **lovely,** whatsoever things [are] of **good report**; if [there be] any **virtue**, and if [there be] any **praise**, think on these things" (KJV).

Reflection:

Now it is your turn. Write a brief note to remind yourself to submit your thoughts to the Word of God, based on Philippians 4:8.

____

____

____

____

Trust the Process

The more we follow the pillars mentioned above, the more our thought life will reflect that of God. The last step in having a positive thought life is trusting God's process. God cannot lie, and His instructions are beneficial to us—that is more than enough reason to trust Him at His Word. A certain level of skepticism is expected from some, but the effectiveness of your journey to a stable thought life lies with having trust and faith in His instructions.

God gives us guidance because there is only benefit in listening to our Heavenly Father. He is omniscient. He knows the beginning and the end. He knows best. So why are we not trusting Him and keeping our thoughts on Him? It's much easier to say it than do. Regardless, we need to constantly exercise divine thinking. Would it shock you to know it's unnatural for us to trust God? Although trusting God does not come naturally for us, it is important to trust Him, because He knows best and has great plans for us. We must train ourselves to trust and submit to God's will over our lives.

"For I know the plans I have for you," declares the LORD, "plans to prosper you and not to harm you, plans to give you hope and a future"
(Jeremiah 11:29, NIV).

Pause: Today, make the deliberate choice to have a positive mindset. No matter what the circumstances are, trust that God is here to protect and guide you. There is no time like this present moment to reframe your thoughts for the highest quality of life and to train your mind to have a positive outlook on life. Now, choose to think thoughts that will give you life, not death.

What Now?

You are at a moment when you are probably wondering, what is the point? If we were all to be candid with ourselves, we would find that there is a void inside us we constantly seek to fill. Our attempts to fill this void occur through unhealthy habits regarding sex, relationships, success, academia, family, children, alcohol, drugs, and many other activities. These unhealthy behaviors occupy this void, reach the ultimate state of happiness, and are often a mirage. Could it be that happiness is a mirage, like an ice-cool glass of water in the middle of a desert? Let us consider the impossible feat of reaching an empirical level of happiness by our own might, and meanwhile consider the infinite possibility of obtaining peace and joy through Jesus Christ. The purpose of restructuring our thought life is to gain access to all of the benefits that come with it. Not only would you have the spiritual reward of an abundant life, promised by Christ Himself, but you would also have physical, psychological, and emotional benefits. Please see below and fill in the blanks.

Benefits of Having Positive Thought Life

Spiritual Benefits	Physical Benefits	Psychological Benefits
❖ Peace ❖ Joy ❖ Love ❖ Goodness ❖ Faithfulness ❖ Happiness	❖ Longer, healthy lifespan ❖ Greater resistance to common illnesses ❖ Reduced risk of death from cardiovascular disease ❖ Lower risk of	❖ Better coping skills during hardships and times of stress ❖ Reduce rate of suicide and overall self-harm ❖ Lower rates of depression/distress ❖ Lower rates of defeated thoughts

❖ Sound mind ❖ Self-control ❖ Many more benefits	developing high blood pressure and diabetes ❖ Reduce or maintain body weight/fat ❖ Many more benefits	❖ Lower rates of anxiety ❖ Many more benefits

PART III
PRUNING

Chapter Three
THE PROCESS

"Everything has seasons, and we have to be able to recognize when something's time has passed and be able to move into the next season. Everything that is alive requires pruning as well, which is a great metaphor for endings."
—Henry Cloud

The act of pruning is a necessary process for growth and health of many things— gardening, spiritual well-being, and growing up. For the purpose of our journey in establishing divine thoughts, we will peel the layers of the spiritual pruning process. The working definition of spiritual pruning for this chapter is the following: a spiritual process by which a person's "flesh" (the physical desires that are contrary to the will of God; the opposite of the spirit) is examined for any damaged or destructive thought process, behaviors, and lifestyles that are displeasing to God. If any are found, they are removed.

For the flesh desires what is contrary to the Spirit, and the Spirit what is contrary to the flesh. They are in conflict with each other, so that you are not to do whatever you want" (Galatians 5: 7, NIV).

The process of pruning the flesh consists of three specific components: finding and analyzing the roots of the flesh, uprooting the infested roots, and replacing them with Godly desires. As we progress in this chapter, rest assured that there is no condemnation when you seek after Christ. God's pruning period is to be implemented with kindness. I strongly encourage you to be gentle with yourself while you are maintaining the highest level of transparency and honesty affirmed by God.

"There is therefore now no condemnation to them which are in Christ Jesus, who walk not after the flesh, but after the Spirit" (Romans 8:1, KJV).

The ultimate goal of undergoing a pruning process is to bear the fruit of life. You can only harvest good fruit by letting go of your own desires and placing your confidence in God.

"But blessed is the one who trusts in the LORD, whose confidence is in him. They will be like a tree planted by the water that sends out its roots by the stream. It does not fear when heat comes; Its leaves are always green. It has no worries in a year of drought and never fails to bear fruit" (Jeremiah 17:7-8, NIV).

How Deep Are Your Roots?

Since my trade is not botany, I am not suited to explain in great depth the anatomy and function of roots. Experts say that some plants' roots can grow more than twenty feet deep. Roots need water, oxygen, and adequate soil depth to grow rapidly and stay firmly embedded. The foundation of your spiritual well-being thrives from the roots connected to God. Either you are rooted in soil that bears good fruit, or you are rooted in soil that does not bear any fruit, like the wayside, rocky, and thorny soil described in Matthew 13:3-6. As you consider the condition of your roots, also consider the depth of your soil. The deeper and stronger your roots, the more elements you will be able to endure. So, how rooted are you, and how deep do your roots travel?

The conditions of our roots are determined by the amount of water, oxygen, and suitable soil in which they are planted. As you understand ways to cultivate your spiritual roots, be intentional in sustaining the state of your soil. First and foremost, make certain that your roots are receiving adequate water. In the context of spiritual growth, water symbolizes the abundance of life we receive from Jesus Christ.

"But whoever drinks of the water that I shall give him will never thirst. But the water that I shall give him will become in him a fountain of water springing up into everlasting life" (John 4:14, NKJV).

Pause:

How rooted are you in Jesus Christ?

____

____

____

Reflection:

If you are unsure of how to answer this question, ask yourself, "How often do I drink from His Fountain?" Jesus promises us eternal life, and he is inviting us to drink from His fountain, which is His Word.

____

____

____

____

The intensity of your thirst for a closer relationship with God and spiritual growth determines the amount of water your roots consume. So, how thirsty are you for the Word of God?

____

____

____

____

Are you drinking from the world's fountain, or from God's fountain?

____

____

____

____

In addition to water symbolizing life, water also signifies growth, prosperity, and a source of security where resources do not run out. Reflect on the passage below:

"Blessed is the man Who walks not in the counsel of the ungodly, Nor stands in the path of sinners, Nor sits in the seat of the scornful; But his delight is in the law of the LORD, And in His law he meditates day and night. He shall be like a tree planted by the rivers of water, that brings forth its fruit in its season, whose leaf also shall not wither; and whatever he does shall prosper" (Psalm 1: 1-3, NKJV).

Pause:

Are you planted by a stream of water or in the desert? Explain.

When your spirit is depleted, whom do you depend on for replenishment?

As you reflect on your life, consider the condition of your roots with unbiased honesty.

Heart/Mind Check:

Share your thoughts on how much you desire God and how your life reflects that.

Do you desire earthly wealth and prosperity more than you desire God? Explain.

When seeking God, do you offer your heart, soul, and mind? If so, how does it reflect in your life? If not, how can you move toward offering Him your heart, soul, and mind?

____

____

____

____

Do you desire intimacy with God, or are you more occupied with what He can provide for you? Explain.

____

____

____

____

There is only one requirement for your roots to grow deeply and rapidly, and that is for you to remain connected to Jesus Christ. Depend on Him for your source of liveliness. In John 15:5, Jesus referred to Himself as the Vine. Just like a branch would need to remain connected to a tree's trunk to remain alive and bear fruit, as Jesus's followers, we also need to remain connected to Him in order for us to remain alive and produce good fruit—Love, Joy, Peace, Patience, Goodness, Kindness, Gentleness, Faithfulness, and Self-Control (Galatians 5:22-23).

"I am the vine; you are the branches. If you remain in me and I in you, you will bear much fruit; apart from me you can do nothing. If you do not remain in me, you are like a branch that is thrown away and withers; such branches are picked up, thrown into the fire and burned. If you remain in me and my words remain in you, ask whatever you wish, and it will be done for you. This is to my Father's glory, that you bear much fruit, showing yourselves to be my disciples" (John 15:5 NIV).

Spirit Over Flesh:

Pruning is strenuous, regardless of the exertion required. However, it should not be avoided. Because the final results render such a work of beauty, pruning should be embraced. The outcome of the spiritual pruning process is fruitful, and guarantees an improvement in one's character as a follower of Christ. As you go through the pruning process in your life, consider the fruit that the spirit will produce: Love, Joy, Peace, Patience, Kindness, Goodness, Faithfulness, Gentleness and Self-Control (Galatians 5:22-23, NIV). As a servant of Christ, exhibiting the fruit of the spirit is profitable for the kingdom, as you will be able to exemplify Christ's characteristics to the world and speak of His glory.

Roots Check:

What fruit are you bearing—the fruit of the spirit or the flesh? Review Galatians 5:19-21: *"The acts of the flesh are obvious: sexual immorality, impurity and debauchery; idolatry and witchcraft; hatred, discord, jealousy, fits of rage, selfish ambition, dissensions, factions and envy; drunkenness, orgies, and the like. I warn you, as I did before, that those who live like this will not inherit the kingdom of God."* (NIV)

____

____

____

____

What part of your flesh are you struggling to remove? As you consider this question, consider **your mind** (impure thoughts, debauchery, selfish ambitions); **your eyes** (pornography, envy, idolatry) **your tongue** (lying, gossiping, speaking death); **your heart** (hatred, discord, jealousy, fits of rage, dissensions); **your body:** (sexual immorality, witchcraft, drunkenness, and orgies, just to name a few).

____

____

____

____

One of the consequences of holding on to our fleshly desires is that we will bear no fruit.

"He cuts off every branch in me that bears no fruit, while every branch that does bear fruit he prunes so that it will be even more fruitful" (John 15:2,

NIV).

Embracing the Pruning Process:

To embrace a painful process requires spiritual maturity. Embracing a process does not mean that we do not struggle; it simply means that we are trusting God to guide and lead us, which is **the first step.**

"Trust in the LORD with all your heart and lean not on your own understanding; in all your ways submit to him, and he will make your paths straight" (Proverbs 3:5-6, NIV).

Pause:

How much do you trust God to lead and guide you in your thought life?

____

____

____

____

How much confidence do you put in God when it comes to Him leading your life?

____

____

____

____

If you were to be honest, would you say that you trust and believe that God is enough for you? Explain.

____

____

____

The second step in embracing the process is to surrender your own desires and accept God's desires. There are areas of our lives that we have a difficult time letting go of. However, we must learn to trust that God's ways are better than our ways.

What fleshly desires do you need to surrender to God?

____

____

____

____

What do you suppose is keeping you from surrendering those desires to God?

____

____

____

____

The third step is being completely transparent with God, who is omniscient. What areas of your life do you honestly want to hold on to, even with knowing it's displeasing to God?

____

____

____

____

The fourth step is to have a positive outlook on the pruning process, trusting that God only wants to perfect your faith.

"Consider it pure joy, my brothers and sisters, whenever you face trials of many kinds, because you know that the testing of your faith produces perseverance. Let perseverance finish its work so that you may be mature and complete, not lacking anything" (James 1:2-4, NIV).

What are your thoughts on James 1:2-4?

____

____

____

The fifth step in embracing the process is to accept that God's plans are best, and that we must learn to seek those plans. It is not enough for us to know that His plans are good for us without seeking after those plans.

"For I know the plans I have for you," declares the LORD, "plans to prosper you and not to harm you, plans to give you hope and a future. Then you will call on me and come and pray to me, and I will listen to you. You will seek me and find me when you seek me with all your heart. I will be found by you," declares the LORD, "and will bring you back from captivity" (Jeremiah 29: 11-14, NIV).

Have you accepted the plans that God has for you? If so, in what way?

____

____

____

____

If not, how do you think your flesh has impeded you from seeking God's plans wholeheartedly?

____

____

____

____

Have you sought to discover what plans God has for you? If not, here is your opportunity.

Prayer: Lord, your Word says to seek you, and I am seeking you. Please guide me. Lead me, and give me the desire to thirst for you. Please give me the heart that seeks after you.

Reminder Verse: *"Then you will call on me and come and pray to me, and I will listen to you. You will seek me and find me when you seek me with all your heart"* (Jeremiah 29:12-13, NIV).

Now it is your turn to write down your prayer asking God to guide and lead you.

____

____

____

____

Confess your hidden sin(s) to your accountability partner. If you do not have one, seek God to connect you with an accountability partner.

Prayer for hidden sins: Lord, I confess that my thoughts have been impure. I confess that my thoughts are not pleasing unto you. I confess that I am comfortable in my hidden sins, since they are unseen and cannot be judged by humans. Lord, forgive me, for I have sinned in my heart, in my mind, in my thoughts, and in my actions. I repent and receive your grace and mercy.

Now it is your turn. Write down a prayer for God to release you from your hidden sins.

____

____

____

____

Review on how to Embrace the Pruning Process:

Step 1: Trust the process

Step 2: Relinquish your fleshly desires and receive God's will

Step 3: Be honest and transparent

Step 4: Have a positive outlook

Step 5: Accept His Plans

PART IV
PERSEVERANCE

Chapter Four
THE REWARD OF PERSEVERANCE

"Patience and perseverance have a magical effect before which difficulties disappear and obstacles vanish."
—John Quincy Adams

Perseverance is people's ability to continue a task with the same purpose that they had when they started, prior to facing obstacles and discouragements. It is to continue, steadfast with the belief and confidence that God, who started the work in you, will see you through completing it (Philippians 1:6). When I think of the word *perseverance*, the parable of the precious widow in Luke 18: 1-8 comes to mind.

"Then Jesus told his disciples a parable to show them that they should always pray and not give up. He said: 'In a certain town there was a judge who neither feared God nor cared what people thought. And there was a widow in that town who kept coming to him with the plea, 'Grant me justice against my adversary.' For some time he refused. But finally he said to himself, 'Even though I don't fear God or care what people think, yet because this widow keeps bothering me, I will see that she gets justice, so that she won't eventually come and attack me! And the Lord said, 'Listen to what the unjust judge says. And will not God bring about justice for his chosen ones, who cry out to him day and night? Will he keep putting them off? I tell you, he will see that they get justice, and quickly. However, when the Son of Man comes, will he find faith on the earth?'" (NIV)

Living Witness to Not Giving Up

One principle I have learned is before you know it, you will [fill in the blank]. I am a strong believer that the work God has started in you will always come to fruition. Before you know it, you will come out of your situation victoriously—if you do not give up. Perseverance is the essence of striving to accomplish what seems to be impossible.

"Being confident of this, that he who began a good work in you will carry it

on to completion until the day of Christ Jesus" (Philippians 1:16, NIV).

From the parable above, Jesus taught us some valuable lessons:

1. Jesus taught us the importance of always praying.

    - ❖ No matter what circumstances we faced, Jesus encourages us to pray without ceasing (1 Thessalonians 5:17). For like the widow, eventually our plea will be granted, if it is God's will.

Reflect:

Are there some prayers you have ceased? Begin to pray them again.

2. Jesus taught us to never give up.

    - ❖ Sometimes, things will not work out the way we planned or hoped. But do not give up; they will work out according to God's perfect plans.

3. Wait on God—He will bring justice for His chosen ones.

"Wait on the LORD: be of good courage, and he shall strengthen thine heart: wait, I say, on the LORD" (Psalm 27:14, KJV).

Would you have continued to plead with the judge for justice? Would you remain consistent in your behavior? Many times, we opt for the road of least resistance, often right before our breakthrough. Every human being enters this world with the ability to dream big. As children, we believe in the impossible; many refer to it as a childlike faith. As we experience disappointments in life—by the way of failures or negative thoughts—we then experience shifts in our mindsets that diminish our childlike faith and give way to defeated thoughts. In order for us to have divine thoughts, we must tap into our childlike faith and start to believe in the impossible again. We must persevere through it all, and believe that we can do all things through Christ who gives us strength (Philippians 4:13).

Believing in the Impossible

Are you ready to experience a magical effect, where all things become possible for you through Christ? Like the precious widow, be determined to persevere through any challenge you encounter, even when it doesn't make sense. Perseverance is a valuable asset as you work toward having divine thoughts. With it, you will push through the defeated thoughts as you train your brain to overcome. The more you practice determination, the more your brain will be conditioned to the tenacity of hardships. The enemy has a way of tricking us into believing that we cannot finish the race. Like a flowing river with countless rocks throughout, the flow of positive, divine thoughts should not cease when the rocks of life are placed in our lives.

As you face adversities, you do not have to fall prey to defeated thoughts. Adversities are simply an upturn on the "bench press" to increase your faith and trust in God. Every challenge is your opportunity to exercise faith and patience. Many of us are familiar with the saying "it's easier said than done." You usually hear this statement when people have a difficult time achieving a particular goal in spite of their efforts, but other people are encouraging them to believe. If this phrase has been part of your vocabulary, I am inviting you to remove it permanently. Believe in the impossible.

"No, in all these things we are more than conquerors through him who loved us" (Romans 8:37, NIV).

The only requirement to persevering through any challenge is to believe that you are not in this alone. God is right there with you, and He only wants you to trust and persevere through it all.

Pause:

Take some time to meditate on these phrases and embrace the fact that you have lived them out. For every breath you take, breathe out these words:

"I could have given up, but I didn't." "I am more than a conqueror through Christ, who strengthens me." "I am stronger than I think.;" "I am still in the race, and God is running right beside me.;" "I am strong and courageous, because of my trust in God."

There are times we read stories of biblical characters, but feel as if they had superpowers because of the era in which they lived, which let them overcome certain obstacles. I would like to share Nick Vujicic's courageous story, which has personally touched my life and encouraged me to persevere through several challenges.

His personal story was so powerful that I took it directly from his website, so I would not miss a word. As you read Nick's brief biography, consider how God can use you with your limitations. Also, consider how you can persevere through your challenges.

To learn more about Nick's ministry, visit https://www.lifewithoutlimbs.org

"If just one more person finds eternal life in Jesus Christ... it is all worth it. You can help me spread this message today!"
Nick Vujicic

Imagine getting through your busy day without hands or legs. Picture your life without the ability to walk, care for your basic needs, or even embrace those you love. Meet Nicholas Vujicic (pronounced VOO-yee-cheech). Without any medical explanation or warning, Nick was born in 1982 in Melbourne, Australia, without arms and legs. Three sonograms failed to reveal complications. And yet, the Vujicic family was destined to cope with both the challenge and blessing of raising a son who refused to allow his physical condition to limit his lifestyle.

The early days were difficult. Throughout his childhood, Nick not only dealt with the typical challenges of school and adolescence, but he also struggled with depression and loneliness. Nick constantly wondered why he was different than all the other kids. He questioned the purpose of life, or if he even had a purpose.

According to Nick, the victory over his struggles, as well as his strength and passion for life today, can be credited to his faith in God. His family, friends and the many people he has encountered along the journey have inspired him to carry on, as well.

Since his first speaking engagement at age 19, Nick has traveled around the world, sharing his story with millions, sometimes in stadiums filled to capacity, speaking to a range of diverse groups such as students, teachers, young people, business professionals and church congregations of all sizes. Today this dynamic young evangelist has accomplished more than most people achieve in a lifetime. He's an author, musician, actor, and his hobbies include fishing, painting and swimming. In 2007, Nick made the long journey from Australia to southern California where he is the president of the international non-profit ministry, Life Without Limbs, which was established in 2005.

Nick says, "If God can use a man without arms and legs to be His hands and feet, then He will certainly use any willing heart!" Nick's latest foray into radio will expand his platform for inviting men and women all around the world to embrace the liberating hope and message of Jesus Christ.

Pause:

What did you learn from Nick's story?

____

____

____

____

What will you do to persevere through life's challenges in spite of the obstacles placed in your way?

____

____

____

____

What do you believe are the benefits of persevering through challenges? Find verses that support this:

Examples: "Blessed is the one who perseveres under trial because, having stood the test, that person will receive the crown of life that the Lord has promised to those who love him" (James 1:12, NIV).

"And not only this, but we also exult in our tribulations, knowing that tribulation brings about perseverance; and perseverance, proven character; and proven character, hope" (Romans 5:3-4, PAR).

____

____

____

PART V
PATIENCE

Chapter Five
THE REWARD OF BEING PATIENT

"He that can have patience can have what he will."
—Benjamin Franklin

More and more, it seems as if we are puppets in a chaotic world ruled by an anxious master with a remote control set on fast forward. Even the restaurants have become clever or not so clever by having us pull up to the side to wait on our order, because having you remain in the drive-thru for an additional sixty seconds is longer than their allotted time, which ruins their benchmark. One of my favorite restaurants that I appreciated because of their great customer service now has employees outside taking orders in the drive-thru line even before we get to the menu. What is the rush? Whatever happened to going through the process of waiting? When did we become so impatient? Patience is not just the ability to wait, but the capacity to remain confident and anticipate a great reward while waiting on God.

If you know me, you know how much I love mangoes—mango juice, mango smoothies, mango-flavored ice cream, mango everything.... I just love mangoes. In 2014, I had a neighbor with an enormous mango tree. The tree stretched so far out that during that particular mango season, dozens would fall right in my yard. God gave me a glimpse of what the children of Israel experienced when they received fresh, daily manna. Let's just say it was not only an incredible mango season for me, but a remarkable year, since I was able to bless other mango lovers with the fruit and freeze the rest for months.

I remember visiting my neighbor and sharing with her how much I loved mangoes and desired to own a mango tree in my own yard someday. She then shared the story about her mango tree of forty-plus years, and how it took years of patience for it to produce fruit. You see, her mango tree was not always fruitful; there were times she had to cut off large branches and sections of its trunk for it to become bountiful. She said it took years of patience and pruning, at times extreme, for her tree to be rejuvenated and produce the abundance of mangoes that I had the pleasure of enjoying.

So what does my love for mangoes and a mango tree have to do with patience? Everything! You see, there are times when we enjoy the fruit of something without fully grasping the process it had to go through to become fruitful. In order for me to enjoy a delicious mango, I must be patient to wait for mango season. Although I can go to the grocery store and purchase one during off seasons, waiting is more rewarding.

"Patience will achieve more than force."
—Edmund Burke

When our desires for an outcome become stronger than our ability to wait, we run the risk of missing out on the beautiful journey God wants us to experience through our waiting process. At times, the very thing we desire can cause us grief. Remember that first kiss you couldn't wait to experience? That spouse you wanted to marry? Or that child you wanted to conceive? Once you finally received those blessings, was it everything you ever wanted? For many people, the answer is no. The first kiss was disappointing or not as fascinating as anticipated. The spouse caused stress and irritability. And the child, well, the child took away all of your freedom and ability to enjoy some peace and quiet. Do not get me wrong, all of these are true blessings to have in their respective places, but when you rush through the process, once received, the result may not be as pleasurable.

I remember feeling extremely anxious and impatient to complete my doctorate degree, and then I finally did! Yippee, yay, I am now a doctor. Everything I have ever dreamt of will now come to pass—wrong! I must admit, once the high wore off, I was left with this unexpected emptiness—which could have been due to the thousands of dollars owed on student loans. In addition to my loans, my life and identity had been tied into my academics—twelve years of primary and secondary education, three years of undergraduate studies, two years of graduate school with my masters, and an additional five and a half years of doctorate studies. So yes, having been in school for over twenty-two years, and rushing through the process, when you finally reach the mountaintop (which some would view that obtaining a doctorate is at the age of twenty-eight), you're left with a lot of mixed emotions and unanswered questions. What just happened? I was six, and now I am twenty-eight. Did I learn anything? What if I am quizzed, and "they" find out I am not as smart as I am expected to be? What if a fifth grader is smarter than me?

So now, my number one advice to people, especially young students and professionals, is enjoy the process!

Enjoy the Process

"Transformation is a process, and as life happens there are tons of ups and downs. It's a journey of discovery - there are moments on mountaintops and moments in deep valleys of despair."
—Rick Warren

I invite you to enjoy the process of life with great anticipation of a wonderful outcome. God is leading and guiding you through it. If you know me, you will always hear me say, "eventually, you will [fill in the blank]." There's no rush in reaching your dreams, as long as you are working toward them. As they say, it is not the destination that counts, but the journey. You are in no competition. If you were in any competition, it would be with impatience—fighting to get ahead of impatience so you can continue to ride the wave, enjoy the breeze, smell the roses of life. In order for you to enjoy the process, you must become comfortable with discomfort and uncertainty. Unless you are a psychic, you will never know the how and when of any process. But with trust in God, you will know, with confidence, that He will accomplish the work in you that He has started (Philippians 1:6).

To enjoy the process, one must be willing to adopt divine, Godly thoughts that will aid in their level of patience. In order to have divine thoughts, one must be able to endure the uncertainty of life. Many grow weary when they are uncertain of an outcome. We are notorious for reciting verses that speak on patience, but applying it in our lives is a different story. I wonder how blessed the people of God would be if we started to exercise patience in our lives? My prayer for us is that we have more patience, so that we can see the glory of God manifest more in our lives. It is not enough to memorize Proverbs 3:5-6 and claim it as your favorite verse; you must believe it and embrace it.

"Trust in the LORD with all your heart and lean not on your own understanding; In all your ways submit to him, and he will make your paths straight" (NIV).

When people begin to lean on their own understanding, they grow weary. This fatigue comes when a person does not completely trust that God is in control of the outcome. In addition to trust, patience requires hope in the Lord to deliver what we do not yet have or see (Romans 8:25). It's easy to practice patience when you have a timeframe, but a great challenge when you have no idea how long you'll have to wait. The Bible offers us great examples of men and women who exercised patience. I will share a few of the scriptures, but first, I would like to share a couple of my personal stories; perhaps you will be able to relate. As I go down memory lane, join me in connecting with your own memories. When there is no other option, choose patience.

I remember growing up in Haiti, watching my family send and receive messages to loved ones in the United States via a tape recorder and handwritten letters. After some time, they then had the opportunity to speak via the telephone. They utilized this process called *teleco*. You would go to the teleco and provide the operator with the number and name of the person you desired to reach. They would then place the call. If the person was not available, you would have to wait for hours—sometimes the entire day—until the operator reached the person. Imagine the frustration and agony of waiting. But hope and anticipation to send a message or hear a loved one's voice superseded the waiting process. There were days when my mother and I had to travel over eight hours from the province area to the city to utilize the teleco so she could call my dad. The fifteen-minute phone calls superseded those long, tiring bus rides, because the joy of hearing from my dad made it worthwhile.

Those of you who did not grow up in a third-world country may not be able to relate to being phoneless, but you may be able to relate to life before unlimited talk, text, and data. I apologize for bringing up this painful process of waiting in your memory. Prior to having my own cellphone, I remember walking to the phone booth to call my crush at the time, for the sake of privacy. The thirty-minute walk felt more like three minutes, due to the anticipation that my crush would be waiting by the phone for my call. But on the days when I received no answer, impatience kicked in. There was frustration, anger, and questioning why he was not available. Can you relate?

Then text messages became available, but there was a costly charge for using it before 7:00 p.m. There was a waiting period during the weekday. Soon after, there was unlimited data, and you were able to reach anyone, anywhere, at any time, if the person was available. The world offers us many quick, convenient things—fast food restaurants, unlimited data, instant messaging, movies on demand. However, what the world cannot provide for us is the virtue of patience that comes from within. The ability to wait through a process without feelings of irritability, but with a calm and hopeful spirit, results in great rewards, and comes only from the Holy Spirit.

Our ability to wait continues to diminish each and every day. In fact, there are some people who are becoming more aggressive through the years. It could be during a traffic jam, and a person constantly blows the horn to get you out of the way; a person who sighs, huffs, and puffs as you place your groceries down for a family of seven; or a person at the doctor's office who goes up to the counter every three minutes to inquire about the expected waiting time. We are very impatient creatures. We are so impatient that we are willing to forfeit the long-term blessings that God has for us for instant gratification.

Pause and Reflect:

When was the last time you found yourself forfeiting God's blessings simply because you could not wait any longer for the things He has promised you?

Mind Check:

Let me rephrase that—when was the last time you forfeited God's blessings because you chose your fleshly desires over His promises for you? Write out the negative effect of your choice.

____

____

____

____

If you had the option to make a decision to receive a small reward by only waiting a short time, versus receiving a greater reward and having to wait a longer period (a few years, or even a decade or so), which would you choose and why?

Reflection:

____

____

____

____

There are times when our minds trick us into believing our waiting period is longer than it actually is. Waiting at the doctor's office for five minutes feels like half an hour, waiting in line at the grocery store for fifteen minutes feels like hours on hours, and being stuck in traffic for thirty minutes sometimes feels like days. Patience is not only a virtue, but also the key that unleashes a chaotic mind and replaces it with peace and a sound mind. Patience allows our fast-paced brain to slow down enough to shut out the noise of the world and hear the Holy Spirit whisper promises to us as He comforts us through the challenges of life.

Reflect:

What are some noises in your life that are getting in the way of you hearing from God?

____

____

____

____

____

Mind Check: If you had the option to continue to experience anxious thoughts versus peaceful thoughts, which would you choose and why?

____

____

____

____

<u>Immense Patience = Faith</u>

Patience also requires faith in the One who places these dreams, hopes, and aspirations inside you. Let us take some time to read Hebrews 11, about how the people of God were able to exercise patience by putting their faith in action. As you read through this passage, consider the lessons you can learn from these people of faith.

Hebrews 11: 1-44, NIV

1 Now faith is confidence in what we hope for and assurance about what we do not see. 2
This is what the ancients were commended for. 3 By faith we understand that the universe
was formed at God's command, so that what is seen was not made out of what was
visible. 4 By faith Abel brought God a better offering than Cain did. By faith he was
commended as righteous, when God spoke well of his offerings. And by faith Abel still
speaks, even though he is dead. 5 By faith Enoch was taken from this life, so that he did
not experience death: "He could not be found, because God had taken him away." Before
he was taken, he was commended as one who pleased God. 6 And without faith it is
impossible to please God, because anyone who comes to him must believe that he exists
and that he rewards those who earnestly seek him. 7 By faith, Noah, when warned about
things not yet seen, in holy fear built an ark to save his family. By his faith he condemned
the world and became heir of the righteousness that is in keeping with faith. 8 By faith,
Abraham, when called to go to a place he would later receive as his inheritance, obeyed
and went, even though he did not know where he was going. 9 By faith, he made his home
in the Promised Land like a stranger in a foreign country; he lived in tents, as did Isaac
and Jacob, who were heirs with him of the same promise. 10For he was looking forward to
the city with foundations, whose architect and builder is God. 11 And by faith, even Sarah,
who was past childbearing age, was enabled to bear children because she considered him
faithful who had made the promise. 12 And so from this one man, and he as good as dead,
came descendants as numerous as the stars in the sky and as countless as the sand on the
seashore. 13 All these people were still living by faith when they died. They did not receive
the things promised; they only saw them and welcomed them from a distance, admitting
that they were foreigners and strangers on earth. 14 People who say such things show that
they are looking for a country of their own. 15 If they had been thinking of the country they
had left, they would have had opportunity to return. 16 Instead, they were longing for a
better country—a heavenly one. Therefore God is not ashamed to be called their God, for
he has prepared a city for them. 17-18 By faith, Abraham, when God tested him, offered
Isaac as a sacrifice. He who had embraced the promises was about to sacrifice his one
and only son, even though God had said to him, "It is through Isaac that your offspring
will be reckoned." 19 Abraham reasoned that God could even raise the dead, and so in a
manner of speaking he did receive Isaac back from death.20 By faith, Isaac blessed Jacob
and Esau in regard to their future. 21 By faith, Jacob, when he was dying, blessed each of
Joseph's sons, and worshiped as he leaned on the top of his staff. 22 By faith, Joseph,
when his end was near, spoke about the exodus of the Israelites from Egypt and gave
instructions concerning the burial of his bones. 23 By faith, Moses' parents hid him for
three months after he was born, because they saw he was no ordinary child, and they
were not afraid of the king's edict. 24 By faith, Moses, when he had grown up, refused to

be known as the son of Pharaoh's daughter. [25] *He chose to be mistreated along with the people of God rather than to enjoy the fleeting pleasures of sin.* [26] *He regarded disgrace for the sake of Christ as of greater value than the treasures of Egypt, because he was looking ahead to his reward.* [27] *By faith, he left Egypt, not fearing the king's anger; he persevered because he saw him who is invisible.* [28] *By faith, he kept the Passover and the application of blood, so that the destroyer of the firstborn would not touch the firstborn of Israel.* [29] *By faith, the people passed through the Red Sea as on dry land; but when the Egyptians tried to do so, they were drowned.* [30] *By faith, the walls of Jericho fell, after the army had marched around them for seven days.* [31] *By faith, the prostitute Rahab, because she welcomed the spies, was not killed with those who were disobedient.* [32-34] *And what more shall I say? I do not have time to tell about Gideon, Barak, Samson and Jephthah, about David and Samuel and the prophets, who through faith conquered kingdoms, administered justice, and gained what was promised; who shut the mouths of lions, quenched the fury of the flames, and escaped the edge of the sword; whose weakness was turned to strength; and who became powerful in battle and routed foreign armies.* [35] *Women received back their dead, raised to life again. There were others who were tortured, refusing to be released so that they might gain an even better resurrection.* [36] *Some faced jeers and flogging, and even chains and imprisonment.* [37-38] *They were put to death by stoning; they were sawed in two; they were killed by the sword. They went about in sheepskins and goatskins, destitute, persecuted and mistreated— the world was not worthy of them. They wandered in deserts and mountains, living in caves and in holes in the ground.* [39-40] *These were all commended for their faith, yet none of them received what had been promised, since God had planned something better for us so that only together with us would they be made perfect.*

This time go back and read it for a more in-depth understanding. Be patient and avoid rushing through what God is trying to reveal to you. Wherever you see the word "faith," think *patience*.

In order to have divine thoughts—thoughts that are of God, thoughts that will unleash the promises of God, thoughts that offer peace, joy, and a life full of abundance—we must have patience to allow God to perfect His will in us and through us. Below, join me in exploring how faith/patience was demonstrated in the lives of these biblical figures who found favor with God.

[1] Now faith/patience is confidence in what we hope for and assurance about what we do not see.

❖ Even when we cannot see the promises of God, if He said it, we must believe and have hope that it will come to pass. With faith and confidence, patiently wait on it.

[3]By faith, we understand that the universe was formed at God's command,

so that what is seen was not made out of what was visible.

❖ We trust that the world is not going to come crumbling down on us, so how much more will we trust that God will not allow those mountains we are faced with to fall on us. Be patient with the God who created the universe. Everything was made by His own hands. He is in control. He is the masterpiece. He is the potter. He is the God of creation. Be patient.

4 By faith, Abel brought God a better offering than Cain did. By faith, he was commended as righteous, when God spoke well of his offerings. And by faith, Abel still speaks, even though he is dead.

❖ Learn to give God your best, even when it is your last. Stop looking at what your neighbors are doing or what they have; just have faith and give God your best. Be patient for God to reward you with the best, as you give Him your best. It's not about your brothers/sisters/neighbors. This relationship is about you and God.

5 By faith, Enoch was taken from this life, so that he did not experience death: "He could not be found, because God had taken him away." For before he was taken, he was commended as one who pleased God.

❖ God will reward you greatly where you will not experience death. While others are dropping like flies, you will be flying like an eagle. Experience the fullness of God's blessings. Be patient; your full rewards may not be on earth, but in heaven. Be patient.

6 And without faith it is impossible to please God, because anyone who comes to him must believe that he exists and that he rewards those who earnestly seek him.

❖ The lower your patience level, the lower your faith level will be. The lower your faith level, the less pleasing your actions will be unto God. Have patience and have faith. God desires for you to please Him even with a mustard seed-size faith or even with a small amount of patience.

7By faith, Noah when warned about things not yet seen, in holy fear built an ark to save his family. By his faith, he condemned the world and became heir of the righteousness that is in keeping with faith.

❖ Will you have the same level of patience as Noah and continue to take God at His word, even when it seems absurd? Wait on God, even if it takes years for His Word to come to pass. He is not a God who shall lie. Be patient.

[8] By faith, Abraham, when called to go to a place he would later receive as his inheritance, obeyed and went, even though he did not know where he was going.

❖ Obedience is better than sacrifice, and obedience requires patience, because you may not always see the fruit until years later. Will you still be obedient?

Pause: Those promises that you are waiting on will come to pass; continue to exercise patience and trust in God.

[9] By faith, he made his home in the Promised Land like a stranger in a foreign country; he lived in tents, as did Isaac and Jacob, who were heirs with him of the same promise.

❖ Eventually, you will get to the Promised Land. But will you be patient enough to wait on God? He is not a God who shall lie; He will always fulfill His promises. It's up to you to remain faithful and patient while you are waiting.

[10] For he was looking forward to the city with foundations, whose architect and builder is God.

❖ I just love this verse. When you're waiting on God, you anticipate the great things He has in store for you. Everything that is from God is great. Are you looking forward to "the city of foundations, whose architect and builder is God"? Or are you doubting what God has in store for you? Your future is bright and beautiful, even in the midst of chaos, because God is the author and finisher of our faith. He is the architect and builder of our future. Don't just wait on the promises—look forward to the promises.

[11] And by faith, even Sarah, who was past childbearing age, was able to bear children because she considered him faithful who had made the promise.

❖ Did I read this correctly? Does this mean God does not operate by our time clock? Yes, this is true—God is not constrained to our human limitations or our "biological clocks." Be patient and wait.

[17-18] By faith, Abraham, when God tested him, offered Isaac as a sacrifice. He who had embraced the promises was about to sacrifice his one and only son, even though God had said to him, "It is through Isaac that your offspring will be reckoned."

❖ Are you willing to give God the very thing you prayed and fasted for? What if God takes back the child, the job, the home, and the blessings He gave you? How will you respond to Him? What if He ask you to offer Him your very best—will you do it?

19 Abraham reasoned that God could even raise the dead, and so in a manner of speaking he did receive Isaac back from death.

❖ Wow, that's faith beyond my imagination. Lord, help us to believe in the impossible. Help us to believe that you are the God who revives and gives life to our dead situations. Lord, increase our faith like Abraham's faith.

20-21 By faith Isaac blessed Jacob and Esau in regard to their future. Believe in others and bless them and their futures. By faith, Jacob, when he was dying, blessed each of Joseph's sons, and worshiped as he leaned on the top of his staff.

❖ Are you open to allow God to use you, even in your dying bed? How open are you to God using you as His vessel? Your talents are for you to share with others. How are you in the area of mentoring and building up others?

22By faith Joseph, when his end was near, spoke about the exodus of the Israelites from Egypt and gave instructions concerning the burial of his bones.

❖ What legacy would you like to leave? As you reflect on that, consider how it will expand the Kingdom of God.

____

____

____

____

23 By faith Moses' parents hid him for three months after he was born, because they saw he was no ordinary child, and they were not afraid of the king's edict.

❖ How are you protecting your child from this wicked, chaotic world? If you do not have a child, how are you protecting those children around you (cousins, nieces, nephews, mentees, etc.)?

24-25By faith, Moses, when he had grown up, refused to be known as the son of Pharaoh's daughter. He chose to be mistreated along with the people of God rather than to enjoy the fleeting pleasures of sin.

❖ Wow, let's read this again. Moses chose a life of discomfort in order to be with his people, which resulted in him rescuing them from Pharaoh. Our greatest impact comes from getting our hands dirty and experiencing life with the vulnerable. Are you willing to do life with "the least of them?"

26 He regarded disgrace for the sake of Christ as of greater value than the treasures of Egypt, because he was looking ahead to his reward.

Pause and Pray: Lord, give us a heart like Moses. I pray that we can regard disgrace for the sake of Christ as of greater value than the treasures of the world. Help us to look ahead to the reward of God, which is heaven.

27 By faith he left Egypt, not fearing the king's anger; he persevered because he saw him who is invisible.

❖ Is God telling you to go and leave your comfort zone? Be obedient, and go not fearing what could be, but trusting the God of the invisible—the one who guides and leads our path straight. Trust Him (Proverbs 3:4-5).

28 By faith he kept the Passover and the application of blood, so that the destroyer of the firstborn would not touch the firstborn of Israel.

❖ Celebrate the things God has done for you. Praise Him for His deliverance. Worship Him for all that He has done and will continue to do for you. The Jews celebrate the Passover. Reflect on all of the great things God has done for you and celebrate Him. Be careful that you are not turning His blessings into a holiday or religious ritual. As they say, celebrate the creator, not the creation.

29 By faith the people passed through the Red Sea as on dry land; but when the Egyptians tried to do so, they were drowned.

❖ Fear not, for your faith will get you through the storms of life. If God was able to part the Red Sea, He is able to move that mountain in your life keeping you down.

What Red Sea would you like God to part for you?

____

____

____

____

If God does not remove the mountain you are faced with or does not part the Red Sea, how will you continue to praise Him and give Him the glory that He deserves?

____

____

____

____

While you are faced with the Red Sea of life, what lessons can you take from it?

____

____

____

____

[30] By faith the walls of Jericho fell, after the army had marched around them for seven days.

❖ What walls are you currently faced with and how have you been dealing with them?

____

____

____

____

March around your walls by praying for God to not only remove them, but to teach you patience, perseverance, and to strengthen you in your walk with Him. Remember, the walls in your life are there to build you up and strengthen your relationship with God. Avoid walking around them, and allow them to be your reminder of the areas of your life on which God is still working.

____

____

____

____

31 By faith, the prostitute, Rahab, because she welcomed the spies, was not killed with those who were disobedient.

❖ How obedient are you in your walk with God? What areas of your life is God not pleased with? What do you believe God is telling you to let go of?

____

____

____

____

32-34 And what more shall I say? I do not have time to tell about Gideon, Barak, Samson and Jephthah, about David and Samuel and the prophets, who through faith conquered kingdoms, administered justice, and gained what was promised; who shut the mouths of lions, quenched the fury of the flames, and escaped the edge of the sword; whose weakness was turned to strength; and who became powerful in battle and routed foreign armies.

Pause:

Take some time to study the scriptures on the lives of these powerful, mighty warriors who answered God's call. What did you admire most about them? What can you learn from them?

Gideon (Judges 6):

____

____

____

____

Barak (Judges 4):

____

____

____

____

Samson (Judges 16):

Jephthah (Judges 11):

David (1 Samuel 13; 1 Samuel 16):

Samuel (1 Samuel):

Choose three Prophets from the Bible about whom you would like to learn more.

35 Women received back their dead, raised to life again. There were others
who were tortured, refusing to be released so that they might gain an even
better resurrection.

❖ Write your thoughts on how this verse speaks to you:

36 Some faced jeers and flogging, and even chains and imprisonment.

❖ Write your thoughts on how this verse speaks to you:

37 They were put to death by stoning; they were sawed in two; they were
killed by the sword. They went about in sheepskins and goatskins, destitute,
persecuted and mistreated— the world was not worthy of them. They
wandered in deserts and mountains, living in caves and in holes in the
ground.

❖ Write your thoughts on how this verse speaks to you:

____

____

____

____

____

____

39-40 These were all commended for their faith, yet none of them received what had been promised, since God had planned something better for us so that only together with us would they be made perfect.

Pause:

What if God told you that you will not receive your heart's greatest desire on earth, but will receive it all in the Kingdom to come? How would you live your life today?

____

____

____

____

____

____

After reading this passage, share five important lessons you have learned.

1. ____
2. ____
3. ____
4. ____
5. ____

Now consider how you will implement these lessons in your day-to-day living.

What are some challenges that may get in your way of implementing these lessons, and how can you overcome these challenges?

So, now what? How can one truly adopt this characteristic called patience? It's so abstract and seems so unattainable. In order to be patient, you must truly believe that God has a great plan for you, plans to prosper you and give hope and a bright future (Jeremiah 29:11). We all trust in someone or something. It may not be God, but every day, we place our trust in that someone or something. We get in our car, trusting that we will get to our destination safely. We eat, trusting that we will not choke. We go to bed, trusting that we will wake up. So, if we can place our trust in all these things, what would it take for us to place our trust in our Heavenly Father, the creator of heaven and earth?

Reflect:

In whom and what, do I place my trust in? Is it God, things, or people?

Whoever or whatever you place your trust in is the one with whom you will be patient with. The only one who will never fail you is God. Place your trust in Him.

"Trust in the Lord with all your heart and lean not on your own

understanding; in all your ways submit to him, and he will make your paths straight" (Proverbs 3:5-6, NIV).

In order to build patience, people must completely surrender their own trust and place it in the One, who can make any crooked path straight.

Pause:

How willing are you to surrender your control and begin to place your trust in God?

____

____

____

____

Patience in Your Season

Just as a caterpillar has to undergo the developmental process of becoming a beautiful, breathtaking butterfly, we too must understand that our spiritual development is a process. A caterpillar does not become a butterfly overnight, and it must go through the necessary stages in order to fully develop its wings. If you would like to fly, allow God to develop patience inside you as you are growing. A beautiful outcome awaits us when we allow God to do the growing inside us.

Impatience bears sour fruits, whereas patience bears the fruit of the spirit

The evolving process may seem crippling, especially when you observe everyone around you flying and flourishing in their season of life. Beloved, I say, keep your eyes on God, who allows the seasons and appoints the times. Everyone must go through their own seasons of life. Your season of peace, joy, and abundance will come. My heart breaks when I see individuals, especially single people or infertile couples, become bitter and envious when others are thriving in their appointed season. So many become impatient in their waiting. In their single season, they anxiously wonder about who their prince charming will be, when will they get married, and how long will it take for their opportunity to come. For some, their impatience grows so strong that they take matters into their own hands and settle for second-best. This is the result for those who were unable to enjoy the state of being single. Some married couples who desire to have a child go through a similar experience. They grow weary through the process of being at the childbearing time of their life and wondering why they have not been able to conceive. Some take matters into their own hands and enter into an adulterous relationship for the sake of conception. These types of behaviors have been occurring since biblical days. Take a look at Sarai and Abram from Genesis 16:1-6.

> 1 Now Sarai, Abram's wife, had borne him no children. But she had an Egyptian
> slave named Hagar; 2 so she said to Abram, "The LORD has kept me from having
> children. Go, sleep with my slave; perhaps I can build a family through her."
>
> Abram agreed to what Sarai said. 3 So after Abram had been living in Canaan ten
> years, Sarai his wife took her Egyptian slave Hagar and gave her to her husband to be his
> wife. 4 He slept with Hagar, and she conceived.
>
> When she knew she was pregnant, she began to despise her mistress. 5 Then Sarai said to
> Abram, "You are responsible for the wrong I am suffering. I put my slave in your arms,
> and now that she knows she is pregnant, she despises me. May the LORD judge between
> you and me."
>
> 6 "Your slave is in your hands," Abram said. "Do with her whatever you think best." Then
> Sarai mistreated Hagar; so she fled from her. (NIV)

When impatience creeps into your life, be careful that you do not settle for second-best.

Reflect:

Identify at least three times in your life when you were impatient and the outcomes were unfavorable.

1. ____

2. ____

3. ____

____

____

List three areas in your life where you are impatient and still require the trust of God.

1. ______________________________

2. ______________________________

3. ______________________________

____

____

What do you suppose would happen if you were to fully trust God and take Him at His word?

____

____

____

____

What do you see as the benefits of being patient with God?

____

____

____

____

What do you believe it would take for you to become more patient with God, with yourself, and with others?

____

____

____

____

If you had the choice to be a caterpillar on his belly, crawling through the dirt of life, versus an eagle soaring in the beautiful, blue sky, overseeing all the possibilities of an abundant life that God has to offer, which one would you choose? Elaborate.

____

____

____

____

Pause:

God is asking you to be patient as he is developing you spiritually, emotionally, physically, mentally, and psychologically. All He asks you to do is wait on Him, and He will allow you to soar like an eagle. Will you wait on Him?

Verses on which to Meditate:

Patience is difficult. At times, it's scary, to the point where some people avoid praying for patience because they believe that God would test them and put them in situations where they would have to exhibit patience, and therefore they avoid it. Below are verses to aid us in becoming more patient.

"Whoever is patient has great understanding, but one who is quick-tempered displays folly" (Proverbs 14:29, NIV).

"Let us not become weary in doing good, for at the proper time we will reap a harvest if we do not give up" (Galatians 6:9, NIV).

"Wait for the Lord; be strong and take heart and wait for the Lord" (Psalm 27:14, NIV).

The Lord is Patient with us:

"The Lord is not slow in keeping his promise, as some understand slowness. Instead he is patient with you, not wanting anyone to perish, but everyone to come to repentance" (2 Peter 3:9 , NIV).

"Therefore, as God's chosen people, holy and dearly loved, clothe yourselves with compassion, kindness, humility, gentleness and patience" (Colossians 3:12, NIV).

"He says, 'Be still, and know that I am God; I will be exalted among the nations, I will be exalted in the earth'" (Psalm 46:10, NIV).

"The Lord will fight for you; you need only to be still" (Exodus 14:14, NIV).

Be Patient with Yourself:

"For his anger lasts only a moment, but his favor lasts a lifetime; weeping may stay for the night,but rejoicing comes in the morning" (Psalm 30:5, NIV).

Waiting Expectantly:

"In the morning, Lord, you hear my voice; in the morning I lay my requests before you and wait expectantly" (Psalm 5:3, NIV).

"Yet the Lord longs to be gracious to you; therefore he will rise up to show you compassion. For the Lord is a God of justice. Blessed are all who wait for him" (Isaiah 30:18, NIV).

CONCLUSION

DIVINE THOUGHTS

Seeking Peace and a Sound Mind in a Chaotic World

"You will keep him in perfect peace, whose mind is stayed on You, because he trusts in You" (Isaiah 26:3, ESV).

What's next? How do I acquire divine thoughts in the midst of a chaotic world? How can I avoid Peter's syndrome while I am in the boat during the storm of life, and instead experience peace? What can I do when the world seems to be upside down? What are my options when my mind is spinning out of control and there is no one to trust? What can I do?

Pause, breathe, and trust God. Believe that God desires for you to have peace and a sound mind. What you can do is trust that the materials written in this book were God's way of telling you that He loves you and He desires for you to have peace. He has me writing this to tell you, "Be still and know that He is God" (Psalm 46:10, NIV). This book was inspired by God, and there were times it was challenging for me to write, because the material is really for me. But He wanted me to share it with you. At one point in time, I took several months' break from writing, because of how much God was circumcising my selfish heart. Now, it is your turn to allow God to circumcise your heart and submerge you in His love, joy, peace, power, and a sound mind.

"For the word of God is alive and active. Sharper than any double-edged sword, it penetrates even to dividing soul and spirit, joints and marrow; it judges the thoughts and attitude of the heart" (Hebrews 4:12, NIV).

As you digest the material you have read, beloved, I encourage you to be gentle with yourself. It takes time to restructure a defeated thought life. However, if you abide in Christ and remain in His Word, He will help you to renew your way of thinking daily. Remember, divine thoughts are attainable. However, it requires a prepared mind, positive attitude, frequent heart checks (pruning), perseverance, and patience. The journey continues as you take the materials written in this book and put them into practice.

How to Acquire Divine Thoughts

- To have divine thoughts is to replace your own worldly, fleshly thoughts with heavenly, Godly thoughts.
- To have divine thoughts is to trust the promises of God, in spite of your circumstances.
- To have divine thoughts is to trust God with all your heart, to lean not on your own understanding, or your own intellect.
- Divine thoughts are pure, even when your flesh is inviting you to have impure thoughts.
- Divine thoughts are true according to the foundational truths of God, even when your emotions try to convince you otherwise.
- Divine thoughts are honorable, even when your experiences tell you otherwise. Even when you have been betrayed by a loved one, divine thoughts invite you to honor for the sake of your peace of mind and your desire to honor God.
- Divine thoughts are beautiful, even in the mist of chaos. Even when the ugly truth is presented to you, even when it hurts to do what's right, stand firm and choose divine thoughts.
- Divine thoughts will see beauty in the most horrendous of crimes.
- Divine thoughts are worth sharing; they are praiseworthy even when it's challenging to speak of life.
- Divine thoughts inspire you to glorify God even through your sufferings.
- Divine thoughts are thoughts that unite, thoughts that please God.
- Divine thoughts are fresh aromas unto God's nostrils.
- Divine thoughts are the calm, serene water flowing down a river that produce peace and tranquility in the midst of turmoil.
- Divine thoughts give life—abundance of life.
- Divine thoughts permit you to forgive your enemies, and most importantly, to forgive yourself.

- ❖ Divine thoughts may not be pleasing to the flesh, but they are beneficial to the spirit.
- ❖ Divine thoughts are thoughts that say God gives and He takes, blessed be the name of the Lord.
- ❖ Divine thoughts say, "Lord, thy will be done!"
- ❖ Divine thoughts say, "Lord, you are in control. I will trust You. You are Alpha and Omega. You are the author and finisher of my faith."
- ❖ Divine thoughts will respond to situations and avoid overreacting. Even when it doesn't make sense to you, you will remember that it makes sense to God.
- ❖ Through the challenges of life, like losing a child, divine thoughts will say, "Lord, you give and you take." If you become unemployed, you will say, "I will trust you, Lord." When you've been diagnosed with an illness, you say, "My body is your temple; heal it and restore it."
- ❖ Divine thoughts overcome the enemy's schemes to kill, steal, and destroy.
- ❖ Divine thoughts offer joy, peace, and comfort beyond understanding.
- ❖ Divine thoughts give you strength to love your neighbor as yourself.

Beloved, this process may not be luxurious, but it is attainable. Divine thoughts are thoughts that need to be meditated on daily. These thoughts are necessary to win this battle in your mind. Through exercising divine thoughts, you will not only learn to manage this chaotic world that we live in, but you will learn to live in this world victoriously.

Prayer:

Lord, I come to you asking you for forgiveness.

I come to you asking you to cleanse me and purify my mind, my thoughts, my ways, and my heart, so that I can replace my defeated, hateful, despicable thoughts with divine thoughts.

Lord, I come to you thanking you, praising you, magnifying your matchless, glorious name.

Thank you for exposing the lies of the enemy to me.

Thank you for revealing my secret sins to me.

Thank you for exposing me to me.

Lord, I come to you asking you to renew my mind daily.

Please Lord, help me to have thoughts that are pure, that are true, that are holy, that are honorable, and that are pleasing unto you.

Help me to have thoughts that are beautiful.

In Jesus's name I pray,
Amen!

Pause:

Your turn. Take some time to read and meditate on Psalm 51. Then, write out your own prayer, confessing your sins, your ways, and your heart to God. Ask Him for a heart like His.

Psalm 51:1-19, NIV

*1 Have mercy on me, O God, according to your unfailing love; according to your great
compassion blot out my transgressions. 2 Wash away all my iniquity and cleanse me from
my sin. 3 For I know my transgressions, and my sin is always before me. 4 Against you, you
only, have I sinned and done what is evil in your sight; so you are right in your verdict
and justified when you judge. 5 Surely I was sinful at birth, sinful from the time my mother
conceived me. 6 Yet you desired faithfulness even in the womb; you taught me wisdom in
that secret place. 7 Cleanse me with hyssop, and I will be clean; wash me, and I will be
whiter than snow. 8 Let me hear joy and gladness; let the bones you have crushed rejoice.
9 Hide your face from my sins and blot out all my iniquity. 10 Create in me a pure heart, O
God, and renew a steadfast spirit within me. 11 Do not cast me from your presence or take
your Holy Spirit from me. 12 Restore to me the joy of your salvation and grant me a willing
spirit, to sustain me. 13 Then I will teach transgressors your ways, so that sinners will turn
back to you. 14 Deliver me from the guilt of bloodshed, O God, you who are God my
Savior, and my tongue will sing of your righteousness. 15 Open my lips, Lord, and my
mouth will declare your praise. 16 You do not delight in sacrifice, or I would bring it; you
do not take pleasure in burnt offerings. 17 My sacrifice, O God, is[b] a broken spirit; a
broken and contrite heart you, God, will not despise. 18 May it please you to prosper Zion,
to build up the walls of Jerusalem. 19 Then you will delight in the sacrifices of the
righteous, in burnt offerings offered whole; then bulls will be offered on your altar.*

AFTERTHOUGHTS

Divine Worth: Your Identity in Christ

Now that you have learned practical ways to obtain divine thoughts, you can embrace your identity as a child of God. Our Heavenly Father has so much in store for you, all you have to do is accept His free gift of love. While writing this book, the Holy Spirit taught me to completely surrender my will over to Him and trust the course on which He has set me. My prayer is that He will do the same for you and more. I pray that you can begin to live with authority as you learn who and whose you are.

Take some time to reflect on your identity in Christ. Remember, you are a child of the Living God! You are complete in Christ; He has made you whole. You are no longer bound by the enemies' schemes. You are free—free from the enemies' oppression, free from sin and death, free from depression, free from anxiety, free from self-doubt, free from anything that has your mind confused. You are alive and well. You are blameless, righteous, and worthy of love. Your mind is free in Christ. You are victorious. You are more than a conqueror; you are stronger than those who are against you. You can do all things through Christ Jesus, who strengthens you. You are God's workmanship, created in Christ to do good works. You are a new creature in Christ. You are an ambassador of Christ. You are the light of the world, you are salt, you are powerful in Christ. You are the head and not the tail. You are above only, and not beneath. You are an overcomer. You are a partaker of His divine nature. You are a chosen generation, a royal priesthood, a holy nation, a purchased people. You are forgiven of all your sins and washed in the Blood. You are significant!

Now it's your turn:

Who do you believe you are in Christ? Meditate on who God has called you to be. Below, you will find a letter written by me, but inspired by the Holy Spirit. After reading it, I invite you to meditate on these truths and write your own letter as God whispers His promises to you.

Dear Beloved,

I love you! Yes, you. I love you in spite of your faults and shortcomings. I love you unconditionally. It was a delight to create your inmost being. I took my time to knit you together in your mother's womb. As I wove you together in the depths of the earth, I smiled seeing your beauty.

Beloved, I love you!

I created you so beautifully and wonderfully. I want you to know that, to accept it and embrace it.

Even before you were thought of by your mother, you were in my thoughts from the beginning of the world.

Oh beloved, you are my prize. With my hands, I molded you and will continue to shape you into my wonderful child.

Never forget how precious you are. You are my pearl. You are my incredible work of art. You are perfect, because you are made in my image. You are my child and my friend.

Let not your heart be troubled; I am with you always. You have been forgiven, and you are alive. I love you unconditionally, and I have great plans for you. "Plans to prosper you and not to harm you, plans to give you hope and a future." All I ask is that you seek me with all of your heart and mind.

For His glory!

MEET THE AUTHOR

Dr. Yolle-Guida Dervil was born in the beautiful island of Haiti, and migrated to Naples, Florida at the age of ten. She is the Founder and CEO at D'Vine Therapeutic Services, Inc., a nonprofit organization providing faith-based psychotherapy to individuals, couples, and families. She is a Licensed Marriage and Family Therapist with a doctorate degree in Marriage and Family Therapy. Dr. Dervil has a great passion to work with those who have been abused, neglected, abandoned and specifically teens with behavioral and identity issues.

She has been working with individuals from different walks of life, including those who have been marginalized. She has extensive experience working with intimate partner violence, individuals with anxiety, depression, and alcohol and substance abuse. For several years, she has worked in the foster care and adoption area, specifically with runaway teenagers who are at high risk of becoming victims of sex trafficking. She is a great advocate for those who are trapped in this horrendous industry by educating the community. She places high priority on love and respect in the therapeutic process. She offers therapeutic services in promoting better ways to manage anxiety and to improve one's personal growth.

Dr. Dervil's mission is to answer the call God has placed on her life: to proclaim good news to the poor; to bind up the brokenhearted; to proclaim freedom for the captives and release from darkness for the prisoners; to proclaim the year of the LORD's favor; and to comfort all who mourn (Isaiah 61). Overall, her aspiration is to empower individuals to become the best that God desires them to be.

Outside of doing therapy, Dr. Dervil loves to serve and mentor at a local group home, go to the beach, read inspirational books, and listen to inspirational music. She also loves to travel and spend time with her friends and family, especially her siblings, nephews and godchildren.